Good Homes
In A
Wicked World

7th Ladies Day

Irven Lee

ISBN 1-58427-071-3

Guardian of Truth Foundation
P.O. Box 9670
Bowling Green, Kentucky 42102

Dedicated
to
Our Daughters, Judy and Sandra,
*who have enriched our lives, giving us
joy for today and hope for tomorrow.*

IRVEN LEE

INTRODUCTION

Many parents, teachers, preachers, and others who touch the lives of young people have done some wonderful teaching of the Bible principles that relate to the home, but there have not been enough lessons on this great theme. The home is a very important unit of society, and souls are lost when homes fail to function as they should. When there is a breakdown in this important unit of society, the very existence and stability of our nation are threatened. The members of the home, the church, the community, and the nation suffer as a result of the lack of regard for the marriage law and other Bible principles that relate to home life.

There are evidently some powerful influences that are eating away at the foundation of the Bible authority that has meant so much to so many successful parents. It is wonderful success when children are trained to walk in the right way of the Lord through the examples, guidance, discipline, and teaching of worthy parents. These parents and their children are the very salt of the earth that helps to season society with a pleasant flavor in the present time. It is high time that we all become concerned when the influences on the university campuses and in the entertainment world become as degrading and vulgar as they are at this present day.

Evolution and other manifestations of unbelief are among the most serious elements of the destructive forces. When men become infidels, they think they are animals, and they then become, as Peter said, "as natural brute beasts." (2 Pet. 2:12.) Those who lack faith fear no day of reckoning, and they suppose that they can sow to the flesh without reaping the harvest. Preaching Christ and Him crucified more effectively would decrease the number of divorces. The wholesome influence of the teaching of Christ is beyond the power of words to express. America has no greater need than the need for growth in faith in God and in the knowledge of His word.

This little book is intended to be practical and useful to every member of the family who is old enough to read on a sixth grade level and to be a blessing to them and indirectly to those who are very small. We hope especially that young people who are approaching the age of marriage, who have not yet made mistakes, will find it helpful in preventing some of the problems which we discuss. If it helps make some families a little happier and some homes more stable and secure, it will be accomplishing the purpose for which it was intended. We realize fully that one little book of this nature will not suddenly remake and save the world, but we have tried to hit one little nail on the head that will strengthen the framework of home life and help somebody somewhere to build a better home. My wife has done very much work in making the book possible, and she joins me in the hope that our efforts have not been in vain.

America is often too busy working, playing, or watching television to have time to read. This is very unfortunate. The printed page offers a great opportunity for teaching. This book is not meant to be read instead of the Bible, but rather in addition to the Bible. We have the genuine hope that these pages can cause some one to so hunger and thirst after knowledge that is so precious that he will do more reading of the Bible, printed sermons, articles in religious journals, and other useful material. "Give attendance to reading." (1 Tim. 4:13.)

There is often much more emphasis given to the externals and to the things that can be bought with money than is given to the spiritual needs of the home, whose influence will last through eternity. Many happy families have not lived in the most expensive houses and have not had the luxuries that the proverbial "Joneses" have. Many children who have had great amounts of money to spend have become thieves and robbers. Some have become fornicators and slaves to alcohol or other drugs. Those who have "precious faith" even though they may be poor in this world's goods are richer by far than those who are choked by the "cares, riches, and pleasures" of this life. (2 Pet.

1:1; Luke 8:14.)

Let us all help one another to push those things "that perish with the using" to the back burner while we bring those things that "pertain to life and godliness" to the front. Happiness is not for sale, and it is not to be found along the road to materialism. We would all do well to ponder carefully the words of Paul to the young man Timothy: "Godliness with contentment is great gain. For we brought nothing into this world, and it is certain we can carry nothing out. And having food and raiment let us be therewith content. But they that will be rich fall into temptation and a snare, and into many foolish and hurtful lusts, which drown men in destruction and perdition. For the love of money is the root of all evil: which while some coveted after, they have erred from the faith, and pierced themselves through with many sorrows. But thou, O man of God, flee these things: and follow after righteousness, godliness, faith, love, patience, meekness." (1 Tim. 6:6-11.) If we listen closely to these things and heed the warnings, we can have richer, fuller personal lives and happier homes in this present world and may look for the eternal reward in the afterwhile.

Irven Lee

TABLE OF CONTENTS

Chapter 1

THE LAW OF MARRIAGE

The law of God relative to marriage is rather simple and easy to understand. Simplicity generally characterized our Lord as He talked. We are told in Mark 12:37 that the common people heard Him gladly. They would not have heard Him gladly if they could not have understood Him. It is beyond our comprehension that One who was with God in the creation and who possessed knowledge as far above ours as the heavens are above the earth could come in the flesh and so speak that the common people could hear Him gladly. They were the ones that were the easiest for Him to reach. He did not reach the high and mighty, and certainly He made no effort to speak only to the high and mighty. He made a special effort to speak to the poor, to those who had had less opportunity in the field of education, and to those who were little in their own sight.

John the Baptist once sent two of his disciples to our Lord to say, "Art thou he that should come or look we for another?" John was in prison through no wrong doing and was likely discouraged. Jesus asked the two disciples to return to John with this message, "The blind receive their sight, and the lame walk, the lepers are cleansed, and the deaf hear, the dead are raised up, and the poor have the gospel preached to them." (Matt. 11:5.) The poor have the gospel preached to them. The common people heard Him gladly.

The law of marriage is simple and easy to understand. It would be a false effort on my part if I tried to make it seem complicated because it is not complicated. The Lord

11

stated it so that the average man, the common people, could understand it. Back in the days when I was teaching school I had the privilege of having a sixth grade Bible class every morning for several years. I never did have anybody in one of those classes who could not understand the law of marriage as it is given in the New Testament. It is not hard to understand, but it is ignored.

"O Lord, I know that the way of man is not in himself: it is not in man that walketh to direct his steps." (Jer. 10:23.) "There is a way that seemeth right unto a man, but the end thereof are the ways of death." (Prov. 16:25.) America today has decided just to lay the Bible on the shelf and ignore what the Lord has said about marriage, fornication, and adultery. Man has decided to do what seems right in his own eyes or that which appeals to his own reason. He seems no longer to know or care that God has given a law to govern his behavior relative to these matters. Fornication and adultery are winked at and no longer considered sins. The wife of the President of the United States has publicly on national television given her approval of fornication for her unmarried daughter. This First Lady is considered an asset to her husband, who, at the time of this writing, is running for election to office. This gives the indication that her fellow Americans approve of her lack of morals as she approves of a lack of morals in her daughter. I am not a politician, and I am neither upholding nor degrading any political party. What is true of one candidate for office may well be true of any one of the others. For instance, there is a very well known man of influence in governmental affairs who very late at night after a drunken party had a wreck which took the life of one of the opposite sex with whom he had no right to be. I do not believe that any one political party has a monopoly on ungodliness.

In the big universities of our day, a professor may stand before a class and recommend trial marriage and premarital sex. The Bible recommends nothing of the kind. It calls such like affairs fornication and adultery. In 1 Cor. 6:9,10, we read, "Know ye not that the unrighteous shall not inherit the kingdom of God? Be not deceived: neither fornicators, nor idolaters, nor effeminate, nor abusers of themselves with mankind, nor thieves, nor covetous, nor drunkards, nor revilers, nor extortioners, shall inherit the kingdom of God." There is no heaven for such. They will

receive no inheritance in the kingdom of God. The sex sins
are listed first in almost any catalogue of sins that is given
in the New Testament. After mentioning other sins in
this list, such as drunkenness, reviling, and extortion, he
singled out the sin of fornication and spent the rest of the
chapter talking about it. He treated it as very grievous
and said, "Flee fornication. Every sin that a man doeth is
without the body; but he that committeth fornication sinneth against his own body." (v. 18.)

The Bible teaching on that soul destroying, home destroying, subject is very clear, but America has decided to
ignore it and openly advocate the loosening of all restraint
and allow men and women to act like animals in satisfying
their basest natures. In universities while a professor in
front of some class may be approving trial marriage and
pre-marital sex, the administration may grant permission
for a young man and young woman who are not married to
rent a room in the dormitory at very little cost so that they
may spend the night together.

I feel sometimes like saying that surely we have hit an
all time low in the matter of morals. Then I read the first
chapter of Romans, and I think that surely we have not
hit lower than that. The world in the past had its periods
of low moral standards. Certainly the world has always
been inclined to go contrary to the counsel and advice of
God.

The Bible is a very precious book. It is the word of God.
In Hebrews 1:1,2, we have these words: "God, who at
sundry times and in divers manners spake in times past
unto the fathers by the prophets, hath in these last days
spoken unto us by his Son." It is very important to us
that God has spoken by His Son, but just now I want to
notice that "God has spoken." He has spoken on many
subjects, and when He speaks we ought to listen. There
are some men for whom I have a very high regard, and
when they speak I like to be there to hear. What they have
to say is worth hearing. How much more so are the things
that God has said. Sometimes I think we act as though
the things He has said are trivial and of little importance.

What God has spoken on any subject is important,
whether it pertains to our soul's salvation, our daily behavior, our worship and service to Him, our duty to our
fellow man, or our various relationships in life. Let us remember that God has spoken in matters that relate to the

home and make it our daily motto to go by the Bible whether we are talking about the woman's place, the man's place, or the child's place. Let the psychologists and the philosophers say what they will, let us believe that what God has said about marriage through His Son nearly two thousand years ago is just as up to date now as the sun and moon are up to date. We do not need to change the law of God, because it is the perfect law. There is a passage in the Old Testament (Deut. 6:24) that I always underline in every Bible I get. It speaks of the commandments and statutes of the Lord as being "for our good always." Now, what God has said on the subject of marriage is "for our good always." If all America would listen to what God has said on just this one subject, we would have happier individual lives, happier homes, happier children, and far less crime.

In the sermon on the mount, in Matthew 5, the Christ made reference to numbers of Old Testament commandments. He repeated them as they were given through Moses. Then He added, "But I say unto you" and raised the standard above that given to Israel. In verses 31 and 32, He said, "It hath been said, Whosoever shall put away his wife, let him give her a writing of divorcement: but I say unto you, That whosoever shall put away his wife, saving for the cause of fornication, causeth her to commit adultery: and whosoever shall marry her that is divorced committeth adultery."

In Deuteronomy 24:1,2, from which Jesus was quoting, we are told, "When a man hath taken a wife, and married her, and it come to pass that she find no favor in his eyes, because he hath found some uncleanness in her: then let him write her a bill of divorcement, and give it in her hand, and send her out of his house. And when she is departed out of his house, she may go and be another man's wife." In answer to the Pharisees who questioned Him on another occasion regarding this precept given through Moses, Christ said, "For the hardness of your heart he wrote you this precept." (Mark 10:5.)

Jesus said, "Whosoever shall put away his wife, saving for the cause of fornication, causeth her to commit adultery: and whosoever shall marry her that is divorced committeth adultery." That is not hard to read, and it is not hard to understand. There are a lot of questions that people can ask that I cannot answer. They come asking

questions after they have become entangled in complicated situations that seem to me to have no solution, and I
do not know what to tell them to do. I could have told
them before they became enmeshed in their difficult
situations what the law of God is concerning marriage. It
is much simpler to talk to people who have not violated
the law and who are trying to avoid the pitfalls than it is
to try to untangle some of the nets that they have woven
around themselves when they did not examine the law
carefully before marriage.

I want to reach young people who are not yet married. I
want to help them to know the law so that they can enter
into their marriages with the understanding that they
must live together until the death of one of the partners.
The law indicates that one cannot put away his wife because she is lazy or is not physically attractive, or because
she has a high temper or because she is not a good house-
keeper. The only way he may do so is for the cause of fornication. It was the Lord Himself who gave the law, and
He has all authority in heaven and on earth. He has bound
it on earth, and neither Congress nor the State Legislature
can change it. The United Nations cannot come up with
some decree that could change it. Now, states may write
other laws that differ from that and put them on their
statute books, but God's law would still stand. It does not
matter what the law of the land may say, the law of God
will still say, "Whosoever putteth away his wife, saving
for the cause of fornication, causeth her to commit adultery." Putting away one's wife for any other cause than
that of fornication brings about a temptation that is almost certain to lead her to commit adultery. It is a normal
thing for her to want a husband, so she is likely to violate
God's law.

In Matthew 19 we have a record of the Pharisees' coming to Jesus and questioning Him, hoping to trap Him in
His answers. They asked Him, "Is it lawful for a man to
put away his wife for every cause? And he answered and
said unto them, Have ye not read, that he that made them
at the beginning made them male and female, and said,
For this cause shall a man leave father and mother, and
shall cleave to his wife: and they twain shall be one flesh?
Wherefore they are no more twain but one flesh. What
therefore God hath joined together, let not man put asunder. They say unto him, Why did Moses then command to

vriting of divorcement, and to put her away? He
to them, Moses because of the hardness of your
uffered you to put away your wives: but from the
beginning it was not so. And I say unto you, Whosoever
shall put away his wife, except it be for fornication, and
shall marry another, committeth adultery: and whoso
marrieth her which is put away doth commit adultery.''

Is this teaching so deep and complicated that only the
intellectual genius can understand it or is it simple enough
that the common man may understand it? Back in Moses'
day Jesus said that God allowed divorce. He also allowed
polygamy and other things because of the condition of the
people to whom the law was given, but from the beginning
He desired that there be one man for one woman. The man
was to leave his father and his mother and cleave to his
wife, and the two were to be one flesh. (Gen. 2:24.) God
recognized that tie as binding. It is His law of nature that
makes the man to be attracted to the woman and the woman to be attracted to the man. There is a powerful God-
given instinct that thus draws them together.

God had a law in Adam's day that the two should leave
their parents and cleave to one another in the holy ties of
marriage, and it was His will that the tie never be dissolved. That law continued in Moses' day; it remains even
in our day; and it will remain until the end of time. God
does not want man to put asunder that which He has
joined together. It is a sin for man to interfere with God's
binding. There is no such thing as a divorce with two innocent parties. It may be hard for there to be a divorce with
one innocent party. So often the one who is called the
innocent party might not have lost the companion if there
had been a different attitude or disposition shown on his
or her part. The one who poses as the injured innocent
party may have driven the companion away and allowed
him or her to be exposed to temptation that proved too
hard to resist.

Jesus said, ''Whosoever shall put away his wife, except
it be for fornication, and shall marry another, committeth
adultery: and whoso marrieth her that is put away doth
commit adultery.'' That is God's law which we must keep
constantly in our minds. It is sometimes hard to accept. I
am reminded of an instance in which a man lost his life because he dared to warn a king about an adulterous relationship. John the Baptist said to King Herod, ''It is not

lawful for thee to have her." (Matt. 14:4.) Herod had taken his brother's wife, and John was bold in renouncing him for so doing. Herod put John to death, but that did not make his relationship with his brother's wife any less sinful. God's law was still the same. It will remain the same as long as time lasts. John did not say, "Herod, if you will let me baptize you, you may keep her as your wife and everything will be all right." No, nothing could make that relationship right in the sight of God. Whether they recognize it or not, sinners are amenable to God's moral laws.

The marriage law is stated repeatedly in the New Testament as though the Lord intended that we find it even if we rarely look inside His book. For the sake of emphasis, let us look at Mark 10:2-12. I suppose this is a record of the same event which we found in Matthew 19. "And the Pharisees came unto him and asked him, Is it lawful for a man to put away his wife? tempting him. And he answered and said unto them, What did Moses command you? And they said, Moses suffered to write a bill of divorcement, and to put her away. And Jesus answered and said unto them, For the hardness of your hearts he wrote you this precept. But from the beginning of the creation God made them male and female. For this cause shall a man leave his father and his mother, and cleave to his wife; and they twain shall be one flesh: so then they are no more twain, but one flesh. What therefore God hath joined together, let not man put asunder. And in the house his disciples asked him again of the same matter. And he saith unto them, Whosoever shall put away his wife, and marry another, committeth adultery against her. And if a woman shall put away her husband, and be married to another, she committeth adultery."

The same law that applies to the man who puts away his wife applies also to the woman who puts away her husband. She has no more legal right in the eyes of God to put away her husband than the man has to put away his wife for any cause. The man and the woman are bound together as they stated in their wedding vows to be faithful to each other until death. When the one man marries the one woman, the relationship is to last for better or for worse, in sickness and in health, until one of them is called away by death. God so ordained, and man cannot change it.

In the passage we noted from Mark 10, Jesus did not mention the exception to the law that He had mentioned as recorded twice by Matthew. He just stated the law without giving any exception. The Lord made the law. He has the right to make an exception to it. We can illustrate this law and its exception by another law that God gave to which He also gave an exception. In 1 Peter 2:13,14, we are told, "Submit yourselves to every ordinance of man for the Lord's sake: whether it be to the king as supreme; or unto governors, as unto them that are sent by him for the punishment of evil-doers, and for the praise of them that do well." The law as here stated is "Submit yourselves to every ordinance of man." No exception is given. In Romans 13:1,2 we have a very similar command given. "Let every soul be subject unto the higher powers. For there is no power but of God: the powers that be are ordained of God. Whosoever therefore resisteth the power, resisteth the ordinance of God: and they that resist shall receive to themselves damnation." If therefore one violates the laws made by the governing powers of the land, he is violating the laws of God. That is God's law relative to the observance of the civil laws. There is however an exception to that law. God made the law, and He made an exception to it. In Acts 4 there is a record of Peter and John as they stood on trial. They were commanded not to preach any more in the name of Christ. Then in Acts 5 there is the record of all twelve of the apostles as they stood before the Jewish Sanhedrin, the highest court among the Jews. The high priest said to them, "Did not we straitly command you that you should not teach in this name?" (v. 28a.) "Then Peter and the other apostles answered and said, We ought to obey God rather than man." (v. 29.) This is the exception to the law. If the law of the land conflicts with the law of God, then "we ought to obey God rather than man."

Now what? Jesus gave the law concerning the putting away of one's marriage companion. He also made an exception to His own law. The exception is not stated in every passage where the law is given. That does not mean that it does not apply today.

The question regarding marriage was asked Jesus by the Pharisees, not for information, but to tempt Him. They had at various times tried to show that His teaching was in contradiction with the teaching of Moses. They tried to entangle, embarrass, or humiliate Him in the presence of His audience that they might destroy His influence. Moses had permitted exceptions to the marriage law. The Pharisees knew the law and the exceptions. They tried to embarrass Jesus into contradicting Moses. He did not fall into their trap. He had them tell Him Moses' law. Then He raised the standard above that of Moses' precept by stating, "But I say unto you," and He gave only one exception to the original law of God.

We have the law stated yet again in Luke 16:18. We will not expect to find anything stated there that is not exactly in harmony with the passages we have already noticed. In fact, we are not surprised when we find the law stated in almost the exact words that we have found before. "Whosoever putteth away his wife, and marrieth another, committeth adultery: and whosoever marrieth her that is put away from her husband committeth adultery." I think that God has given other laws that relate to marriage and to the making of a happy marriage, but we can well say that the law we have just noticed is the one law relative to the breaking of the bond.

This law should be read to our sons and daughters and to all the young people of the land many times as they approach the age when they begin to think of choosing their marriage companions. If they hear it a thousand times before they are old enough to marry, perhaps they will be better able to make marriages that will stay together. It needs to be taught again and again in every Bible class, in every home, and in every pulpit. If it is taught often enough, at least the young people will know the law and hopefully they will respect it.

One day I was visiting in a hospital with a young lady to whom I had been preaching for some time. Her mother was a member of the church and faithful in attendance. The daughter had been coming to the services for several months. She asked that I sit and talk with her for a while if I were not in a hurry. I assured her that I had time to talk. She said, "You know that I have been coming and hearing you preach. I know I should be a Christian. Especially am I conscious of that now that I have my little boy."

She paused, and then she said a very startling thing. She said, "You may not want to baptize me."

Now, I like very much to baptize people, especially

some one who seemed as sincere and honest as that young lady. I quickly said, "Why?"

She replied, "My husband has another wife, who is living."

Now, I want every reader to give close attention to her next statement. She said, "I didn't think anything about it before marriage, but I certainly think a lot about it now."

That intelligent young lady had lived for approximately twenty years in the house with a mother who was a member of the church, and she married without thinking of the marriage law. The very idea! Now, later, as the young lady grew older and had a child around her feet, she was thinking of the law that she feared she had violated some years before. How did the mother feel? Dear Reader, let me beg you not to let a boy or girl live at your house for twenty years without thinking of the law that is stated so often and so clearly in the Bible. Should not any mother feel a sense of guilt that she had not at least made an effort to warn her daughter of the seriousness of the step she was taking? As one grows closer to the day of death, I should think that she would think still more about the law of God. That would surely make one uncomfortable. If you had a tack in your shoe, it would become more and more uncomfortable the longer you walked on it, and it would never grow easy. A whole lifetime is a long time to have a tack in your shoe!

Young people should be spared the sorrow that is attached to such a situation as I have described. They should be taught early so that they may know and respect the law of God regarding marriage. Then they should be warned quickly if they begin to show a preference for the company of one whom it would be a sin for them to marry. After the tie is formed, it is too late to do much teaching. It is much easier to avoid the danger than it is to escape when once the bonds have been sealed.

In the seventh chapter of Romans the writer is not talking primarily of the law of marriage. Rather he uses the marriage tie to illustrate the relationship between the old covenant made through Moses and the new covenant made through Christ. He shows that a Jew can now be a Christian, not offering the animal sacrifices and keeping the Jewish feasts, and he may have a clear conscience because the old law is dead. It has been nailed to the cross, and Christians are married to Christ. Let us examine the passage. (Rom. 7:1-4.) "Know ye not, brethren, (for I speak to them that know the law,) how that the law hath dominion over a man as long as he liveth? For a woman which hath a husband is bound by the law to her husband so long as he liveth; but if the husband be dead, she is loosed from the law of her husband. So, then if, while her husband liveth, she be married to another man, she shall be called an adulteress: but if her husband be dead, she is free from that law; so that she is no adulteress, though she be married to another man. Wherefore, my brethren, ye also are become dead to the law by the body of Christ; that ye should be married to another, even to him who is raised from the dead, that we should bring forth fruit unto God."

How long is a woman bound to her husband? As long as he lives. What if he is dead? Then she is free from the law of her husband, and she has the right to remarry. Death dissolves the marriage tie, and it is the only thing that can dissolve it without there being sin on the part of one or both of the marriage partners. When death has dissolved the marriage, the woman is not an adulteress if she chooses to remarry. The husband or the wife who is left after death has taken the companion is free to remarry, but mistakes are often made in choosing a new companion. I think that a twenty year old man may use as much wisdom and judgment in his choice as a man of sixty. The man of sixty may remarry very quickly following the death of his wife because he is lonely. He has been dependent on his wife for companionship and cannot reconcile himself to living without her. He acts hastily and unwisely in many cases. There are problems to face, and discretion should be exercised, but when the right choice has been made the second marriage may be as happy as the first, and the Lord may bless the union. Marriage in such case is honorable and desirable.

In 1 Corinthians 7:39 the Lord gives advice to the wife which she should carefully notice. "The wife is bound by the law as long as her husband liveth; but if her husband be dead, she is at liberty to be married to whom she will; only in the Lord." In this chapter, Paul had advised that because of the present distress the unmarried would do well to remain unmarried. It was a time of great trial and persecution, and those who were married and had family responsibilities were suffering greatly. Thus, in an effort to spare the young as much suffering as possible, he advised them not to marry. Yet even in such circumstances as he described he said it would not be a sin for them to marry. The widow was also at liberty to marry, and her freedom was unlimited as to the companion whom she might choose with one exception—"only in the Lord." Judgment and common sense might make other exceptions. To illustrate: it might be unwise to marry one of another race, of another social or financial background, or of a different age; but so far as the stated law of God is concerned she is at liberty to marry whom she pleases—"only in the Lord." If she is sure that the Lord approves her marriage, then she has made a wise decision.

In Ephesians 5:31, Mark 10:7, and Matthew 19:5, there is a statement that is quoted from Genesis 2:24. It is a law as clearly stated as the other laws regarding marriage that we have noticed. Evidently, since it appears so many times in the Bible, the Lord meant for us to notice it and be sure to respect it. It says, "For this cause shall a man leave father and mother, and shall cleave to his wife: and they twain shall be one flesh." A man is to "leave" his father and mother. That is stated as clearly as "and cleave to his wife." The tie between the parents and the child is very close, and it should be, but there comes a time when the young man has not only the right but heaven's encouragement to leave his father and his mother and establish a home of his own. That does not mean that he must cease to love and honor his parents. It is not rebellion. He may feel a greater understanding of them and a deeper respect for them, but he is now ready to be the head of a new home, and he sustains a different relationship to his parents.

At our house we did not have sons, but we had two daughters. The time came when the older of the two finished high school and was preparing to go to college. My wife was very busy making extra dresses for her and doing the many other things necessary to have her ready at the proper time. Now and then a tear would fall as she worked. One day as she was busy near a window she saw a bird's nest which had several young, full feathered little birds in it. The mother bird came, bringing food to them. Then she got in the nest, and with her wings and beak she pushed the young ones out of the nest. They fluttered and protested, but out they went. Then they discovered that they had wings of their own and could fly. They did not need to be dependent on the mother any more. My wife saw a picture of herself and felt that she was pushing her little one out of the nest as she prepared to send her away to school. Just so, when a son marries, he is to leave his father and mother and make a nest of his own. It is true also of the daughter. If she is not willing to leave her parents, she is not ready to marry.

Chapter 2

PREPARATION FOR MARRIAGE

People generally will marry. Some will be prepared for such a step, and some will not be. Whether they are prepared or not, most people will marry. There is a law of Nature which causes men and women to be attracted to one another. God so planned. Marriage is honorable in all, and it is recommended in both the Old and the New Testament. In the very beginning when Adam had been created, God said, "It is not good that the man should be alone; I will make a help meet for him." (Gen. 2:18.)

Paul, who is slanderously reported by some as being opposed to marriage, said, "I will therefore that the younger women marry, bear children, guide the house, give none occasion to the adversary to speak reproachfully." (1 Tim. 5:14.) An elder, who is to oversee the flock of God, is to be the husband of one wife. Celibacy is not the better state. The wise man of the Old Testament period said, "Whosoever findeth a wife findeth a good thing and findeth favor of the Lord." (Prov. 18:22.) The price of a good woman, who would be a good wife, is far above rubies.

A failure in marriage means the breakdown in the home, which is a vital unit of society. Unwise marriages make it very hard for those involved to find happiness here on earth or in heaven after this life is over.

There are some easily understood guidelines that can help in the preparation for marriage. Plans for this partnership should be made with much care and prayer. When a man thinks of becoming a doctor, he knows that there is a long period of preparation before he is able to practice medicine. Such would be true of any other profession which a man might choose. Marriage is one of the most serious steps one can take, and yet too often it is under-

24

taken with no preparation and with little knowledge of the responsibilities that belong with it. Just as it is possible to prepare for one's chosen field of work, it is also possible to prepare for married life. There is a sense in which no one can actually be prepared for all the responsibilities of marriage, but one must recognize the fact that there are such, and he must be willing to face them as they arise and do all in his power to meet their challenges.

The preparation for marriage should begin very early in life; so the parents are very much involved in the matter of seeing that their sons and daughters are trained to be good husbands and good wives. Boys and girls who grow up in homes where the parents love each other and have faithfully taken the responsibilities that belong to them have a far better chance of having happy marriages than those who grow up without having good examples set before them.

The calendar has something to do with the preparation for marriage. In other words, marriage is for adults. There are many young people who marry when everybody around them knows that they are not old enough. I cannot, of course, set a certain age when one is old enough and say that that is the proper age for every one. A hundred years ago when nearly everybody worked on the farm and most of the work was done by hand, the children may have matured at an earlier age than in our day. They did not spend much time in school, and from early childhood they had to work right beside their parents in the house and in the field. The older girls in the family often had the care of younger brothers and sisters while they themselves were only children. They learned very early how to cook, sew, wash, iron, and do many other things of home life. A daughter brought up under such circumstances would be able earlier to assume the responsibilities of marriage and a family than a girl who had done nothing in the home and had depended on her mother for the care even of her own clothes.

Likewise, a son who had been brought up working in the field with his father from the time he was old enough as a child to follow would be able by the time he reached teenage to do a man's work. In his experience in hard labor as he helped to eke out a living under difficult circumstances he would have gained experience that matured him much earlier than if he had spent his days in school and his spare time doing nothing more productive than tinkering with an old car or speeding down the road on a motorcycle.

I cannot set the calendar age because it is not the same for everybody. Much would depend on the circumstances, experiences, and attitude of the couple involved. The young lady who does not know how and is not willing to cook, care for the house, and be a help meet for her husband lacks the maturity necessary for a successful marriage. The young man who has no training in making a living and lacks the good disposition necessary to holding a job is not ready to provide for a wife and children. I am not discouraging marriage, because it is honorable in all; but I would advise children to wait until they are old enough and mature enough to bear responsibility before assuming the role of adults.

I heard a newsman say recently that almost half of the teenage marriages in our country now end in divorce. I am sure that a good number of those that do not end in divorce come very near to it and could not in any way be considered happy marriages. If half of such marriages are going to fail, that is a poor risk for young people to take. Parents, you have a very grave responsibility in teaching your sons and your daughters what lies ahead of them in marriage and preparing them for it.

If there could be some way to elevate the standard of moral conduct in our country, there would be fewer teen-aged marriages. So many of the middle teenaged weddings are followed by the birth of normal, healthy, well developed babies in four or five months. Morals play a great part, and it is no wonder that these marriages fail. They do not have much chance of success from the very first.

A good name is part of the preparation for a good marriage. Indeed, a good name is rather to be chosen than great riches. Boaz could say of Ruth, "All the city of my people doth know that thou art a virtuous woman." (Ruth 3:11.) It is that type of woman who is worthy of and is likely to obtain the right kind of husband. She would not even be attractive to the wild, unrestrained young man. He would look for one of his own kind who would share all the reckless behavior in which he takes part. If ever there is a time to sow "wild oats," it is not in that precious decision-making period of youth. It is not during that period when one is looking for and is likely to find one to marry. I used that expression "sowing wild oats" once in a sermon. We all understand the meaning. A fine elderly lady came to me afterwards and said, "Bro. Lee, you did not mention that with wild oats, you just have to sow them once. They come up next year by themselves without being sown." She was right. You just sow them one time, and you reap harvest after harvest after harvest. "Whatsoever a man soweth, that shall he also reap." If one does not want the wrong kind of harvest he must not do the wrong kind of sowing.

A young man will choose a wife from the crowd with whom he associates. If he is pure and clean and if his associates are pure and clean, then he will choose one for his life's companion who is worthy to share his life. If, on the other hand, he is vulgar and cheap and his constant associates are the same type, he will not even have the acquaintance of a good, clean, pure girl, and therefore he will have no chance to choose one for his wife. "Be not deceived; God is not mocked: for whatsoever a man soweth, that shall he also reap. For he that soweth to his flesh shall of the flesh reap corruption; but he that soweth to the Spirit shall of the Spirit reap life everlasting." (Gal. 6:7,8.) The reaping may continue many decades after the sowing. The devil himself is the author of the idea that a young man must sow his "wild oats." The Bible teaching is very different. It says, "Remember now thy Creator in the days of thy youth." (Ecc. 12:1.) The youth, who thinks that drunkenness, fornication, and other forms of ungodliness are the smart things to do in order to have a "good time" and to be popular with the crowd, is not likely to find himself happily married when he is an adult. Such a young man is destroying all hope of a happy marriage. God knows what is best for us at every age of our lives, and He never recommends ungodly behavior at any time.

Parents are failing in their duty to their children when they fail to bring them up in the nurture and admonition of the Lord. It is hard for parents to provide the right kind of example before their children and give them the proper teaching at home when all around them are evil influences to counteract the home training. Parents themselves are not all doing the things they should do; so often the children are left with neither teaching nor example to guide them in their serious preparation for marriage.

A young man with the drink habit will often promise a

young lady who has taken his fancy that if she will marry him he will give up his bad habit, settle down, and be a good man. Many young ladies have been deceived by such a promise. If a man drinks in spite of the pleadings of his mother, in spite of friends who try to help, and in spite of the teachings of Christ, he is not likely to stop when he wins the girl he wants. His promise is worthless. A young lady may marry him on the strength of his promise and perhaps of his assurance that nobody has ever loved him and understood him. He promises that with her to understand him he will have no trouble giving up his bad habits. Poor blind, deceived girl! If she goes ahead and marries him, no doubt in the face of warnings from those of her relatives and friends who love her, she will be in a poor position to complain about her hardships in having to live with an alcoholic. If she could use good judgment and listen to the advice of others who are in a position to advise, she could spare herself many sorrows and tears. Her problem may have arisen from the fact that she looked in the wrong crowd at the first for her companion. The best marriage companions do not come from the dance halls or the taverns.

So, one of the best ways to insure a happy marriage is to remain always in a good environment. Choose your closest associates from those who have high ideals and worthy motives. Be the kind of person who will attract the pure and clean friend.

We have already mentioned the great responsibility that rests on parents in giving their children the proper teaching and examples. Children who are most fortunate and who have the best chance to have happy homes when they are adults are those who have had happy childhoods in the company of faithful Christian parents. Such children grow up knowing what a happy home is. They know what to look for and plan toward for themselves because they have seen it in the home with their parents. It is very unfortunate that many children do not have this rich experience. They cannot choose their own parents.

Young people who do not have happy childhood homes may find a great urge to marry early in order to get out of an unhappy situation. The desire to escape from an unholy environment is commendable, but so often because of the ungodly parents, they may have been limited in their association with good young people. The right kind of young man or young woman would not care to go frequently into such a home as the one from which they are eager to escape. The early marriage will likely be like the old saying about jumping out of the frying pan into the fire. It is such a sad thing to see the young lady who has never had a happy home marry one who is as unworthy as her father so that her whole life span must be spent in miserable circumstances. The hasty, desperate plunge from one unhappy state into another is costly. She may have grown up in the presence of unkindness and bitterness, and so is tempted by the smooth flattery of some man only to learn soon that he is as ungodly and as unkind as her father from whom she was escaping.

Some excellent young people whose fathers made life miserable for them because of the drink habit or other evil habits have endured the situation until they were old enough to get out on their own and establish good names for themselves while they earned their own living. They can then form acquaintance with other young people who have good characters. From these worthy associates they can then choose life companions who will help them make homes far different from the ones in which they grew up.

Young people, do not marry a stranger. That stranger you meet may be a worthy person or he may be a hypocrite. You cannot tell in a few minutes association. He may be out of prison on parole. He may have another wife. You may think that these are rude remarks to make about that charming stranger that you have just met who is so friendly, but many have been deceived and have been ruined by making hasty marriages without knowing anything about the background of the ones they married. The skilled banker will not make a loan to a stranger. He does not trust his judgment based on appearances, and he is thinking only of a matter of money. Marriage is a far more important matter, and it is for life.

A young man is not prepared to marry until he is able to make a living. "If any provide not for his own, and specially for them of his own house, he hath denied the faith, and is worse than an infidel." (1 Tim. 5:8.) The young husband has the responsibility of providing for his wife. He should not marry if he cannot or will not provide for her. He should be taught that lesson from early childhood. His responsibility may soon broaden out beyond just that of providing for his wife. There will likely be children who must have his support. Then there may be a widowed mother who needs his help. Caring for one's own may include more than just caring for those who live in his house. There may be relatives who look to him to supply their needs. Within the family is the first place that he begins to show piety. We have a proverb which says, "Charity begins at home." That is very true unless it is abused. One's first duty is to those of his closest relatives, but so long as his means will allow he is to share with more distant relatives as well.

When the children come along, there will be added responsibilities for both the husband and the wife. The young mother may resent having a child to take up her time and tie her down at home. The young husband may resent the time that the child takes of the mother which she has been directing to his interests. They both should be well trained to recognize the responsibilities of parenthood before they are married. If they are not willing and able to provide the things the child needs, they do not deserve to have a child. There will be much work and many sleepless nights to endure as well as the time involved; so a young lady is not ready to marry until she is willing and eager to make the necessary sacrifices for a family.

We often hear the expression, "Cleanliness is next to godliness." That is not from the Bible, but I am not sure that the principle is not in the Bible. The young lady who does not know how to keep a clean house is not ready to marry. Too many girls in our society do not so much as make their own beds or clean the floors in their own rooms. They take no responsibility in helping with the housework but depend on their mothers for everything, often complaining when they are asked to do anything in the house. Obviously, these young ladies are not ready to marry. I know when Paul instructed young women to guide the house and to be keepers at home that he had more in mind than sweeping the floors and washing the dishes. Yet those things are important. Some young women seem surprised to learn after marriage that there are meals to cook, beds to make, floors to clean, and laundry to do. Heretofore she has had plenty of time to curl her hair, polish her fingernails, and listen to the radio. It is often a rude awakening to learn that there are other things to do.

Young people, if you would like to have the ideal home, then both partners should be Christians. That is the very first step in beginning the good life together. I am not saying that there would be no problems to arise if both were Christians. No, not that. There are problems that arise in every home regardless of how fine the members are, but a couple has a far better chance of solving those problems if they are both trying hard to live by the teachings of Christ and if they have Him as the very center of their lives. When you find a young man and a young woman who love the Lord and have a high regard for His wisdom and His word, you will find a couple who is ready to take on the responsibilities of married life. They can grow closer together as they study His word together and try to pattern their lives by the principles they read.

If you want to be prepared for marriage, young friend, then become a Christian as soon as you learn your duty. Read and study His word every day. Pray without ceasing. Seek His counsel and guidance in everything you do. You will be rewarded with your heart's desire. Be the best person you are capable of being, choose the right associates, and take your share of the responsibilities while you are still at home with your parents. Not only should you be a Christian yourself to have a good home, but you must marry a Christian. The Bible says, "Be ye not unequally yoked together with unbelievers: for what fellowship hath righteousness with unrighteousness? and what communion hath light with darkness?" (2 Cor. 6:14.) Do not marry into a situation where your righteousness must be in contact with his or her unrighteousness, because there is no communion. Your light may go out in the midst of his or her darkness. Think carefully of these things before making your final decision.

One is not ready to marry who has not learned that the marriage union must last until death. It is a lifetime arrangement. In our day there has come a breakdown in the home relationship because the marriage partners do not enter into it with the knowledge that only death must be allowed to break it. Too many enter into marriage as did an uncle whom I admired so very much when I was a child. He lived for a time at our house and was my hero. He went away to the industrial north to work and soon married a little lady he had known for only a brief time. His oldest brother was doubtful about the marriage because he knew they had known each other too short a time. He also knew the unstable nature of his young brother. He asked him, "What if it doesn't work out?" My young uncle replied, "If it doesn't, it is a big world. I'll take my hat." As you may be able to guess, it did not work out. He took his hat and left, but the world was not big enough to get away from the burden of the responsibility he had assumed and then shirked. He had not been taught or he had not listened to the teaching that marriage is for life, "till death do us part."

One needs to know even when problems arise that the marriage must last. There will be problems. There will be differences in judgment. It is human to err, and all husbands and wives are human. They must both learn to say, "I am sorry. I was wrong." There will come times when first one and then the other must forgive and show mercy. They must each realize that the problems must be solved and solved quickly to save the home. We often hear some one say that marriage is a 50-50 proposition. Not so. Sometimes it is a 75-25 or a 90-10. Sometimes both are wrong, and both need to humbly beg forgiveness and start all over. Paul was not talking about marriage in particular when he made this statement, but it well applies. He said, "Let not the sun go down on your wrath." (Eph. 4:26.) There are problems which arise in any occupation that a man would choose, but he does not quit his job every time something discouraging arises. He tries to solve the problems and go ahead to be the very best worker he can be under the circumstances. Just so in marriage. Each companion should be the very best he or she can possibly be in every circumstance that arises and learn to take the bad with the good. The marriage is to last in sickness and in health, for better and for worse.

In looking for the proper person to marry, remember, young people, that you are looking for just one. You can afford to be very particular and take plenty of time to find the right one. If you are looking for the very best, you will not have as many from whom to pick as you would if you were willing to settle for one of the common herd. If you are looking for one who is standing head and shoulders above all around him spiritually, you must be the kind of person who also stands tall spiritually in order to be attractive to him when you find him. I had a Political Science teacher one time who suggested if one would be popu-

lar he must learn to out-conform the conformists. That is
the way to be popular with the crowd, but that is not the
way to please God or to attract that worthy young friend
whose attention you are trying to gain. The character of
the popular crowd is far below the standard you must set
for yourself if you want a good home with a good
companion.

Mothers should begin instilling into the minds of their
pre-school children that they must be Christians when
they grow up and that they must marry Christians. That
is not too early to begin the teaching. They must teach
them to choose good companions in school and then later
in the business world and finally in the home that they will
one day make. We become like those with whom we associate. Paul told the Corinthians, "Be not deceived: evil
communications corrupt good manners." (1 Cor. 15:33.)
The American Standard Version reads, "Evil companionships corrupt good morals." We tell a great deal about
ourselves by the company we keep. People group together
because they have common interests and they delight in
one another's company. They enjoy going to the same
places and doing the same things. Mothers, teach your
sons and daughters while they are very young to choose
the sort of friends who will exercise a good influence over
them and help them be better persons rather than be a
hindrance to them.

What type of home do you want? Are you truly a Christian with a special desire to please God and succeed spiritually? If so, you will look for a companion with the same
ideals. Would a devout Christian ever deliberately plan
marriage with a worldly person who has no reverence for
God? Surely it must be in a time of weakness when the
Christian agrees to such an arrangement. Similarity of social, economic, and racial backgrounds would be a wise
thing to consider. God has not made laws regulating such
matters, but He expects each person to use wisdom and
proper judgment.

Children are to be brought up in the nurture and admonition of the Lord. One who realizes this and gives
thought to it will want a companion who can share with
him in that great task. Children belong in the home, and
both marriage partners should desire them and be willing
and eager to face the responsibilities that go with them. A
Christian cannot afford to marry one whose example in

word or deed would be contrary to the will of Christ in regard to the bringing up of children. This is quite easy to see if one is using wisdom and is thinking ahead. Indifference on the part of one parent to religious training is very serious. Training a child in the way he should go is both difficult and important. One irreligious parent can often defeat the efforts of the other parent in trying to provide that training.

Good marriages are made from good materials. A good house cannot be built out of slabs from the saw mill. Good homes cannot be built out of poor character.

Love and lust are not the same. There can be a physical attraction at first sight, but love grows with time and cultivation. Flattery is a tool of the god of this world, and he may blind the eyes of an otherwise intelligent person by the use of this dangerous weapon. Some have said that love is blind. Not so. It is lust that cannot see straight. Love can see and admire that which is worthy. Wisdom can discern between the foolish and the sensible. Stop, look, and examine the drawing power in the attraction you feel for that one of the opposite sex.

I, for one, join with those who oppose unlimited freedom for the very young boys and girls to go where and with whom they please, to return when and if they please. There are too many temptations and dangers along the way when there is no guidance. The sex instinct is becoming very powerful and they lack wisdom to know how to control their feelings, so they often begin at a very early age to flirt with sin and invite lust. I wish that parents, teachers, and all others who touch the lives of these young people could keep a loving eye on them and loving arms around them to shield them from sin until they are old enough and wise enough to control themselves.

There is a period which we usually refer to as courtship. It is the springtime of life and can be just as beautiful a time in the lives of two worthy young people as the spring of nature that follows the winter. Every period of life has its special beauties and compensations if we are of a mind to look and if all things are in harmony with the will of God. The tiny newborn infant is a bundle of joy and delight to all around, as relatives and friends gather to watch his changing expressions and the normal motions of his body. Each period in his development brings beauty and joy of its own. Such is always true if the child is growing normally, both physically and mentally. There should be no change in the story when one reaches the age when he is about to become an adult in the full sense of the word and is ready to assume the responsibilities that come with adulthood.

The young man who has developed both physically and mentally until he is a young adult is attracted to a beautiful young lady as certainly as the bright red cardinal becomes interested in the dull brown mate in the springtime. The period of courtship is the springtime of life, and spring is beautiful. Just as relatives and friends can share the joys of a newborn baby and the changing phases of the growing child, just so they should be able to share the delights of a young couple making plans for a life together. When a young man who shows respect for his parents and neighbors and reverence for God begins to take notice of a young lady who is known for her chastity and her meek and quiet spirit, which are of great price in the sight of God, their whole circle of friends smile with delight. What could be wrong with this friendship and developing love? Did not the loving Creator plan that there should be such attraction? It can be a time of rejoicing for parents, relatives, and friends. Springtime has come to two more of the Lord's young saints.

This age in life loses its beauty and luster when improper conduct is shown by the young couple in love. When the lack of proper restraint shows up and lust is substituted for love, it becomes a period of grave danger. There are desires that call for satisfaction, and they are God-given, but, as is true of everything that God has given to each person and to the earth, they can be abused or misused. Can the two not wait for the fulfillment of those desires in the proper way that God and His saints approve? (Heb. 13:4.) It is very sad that some young people are not given any preparation for this period of courtship. They are rather taught that they are like the animals in the fields around them, having evolved from a one-celled beginning along with the animals. Lust and instinct are their only guides. The beauty of holiness is not there. Christians realize that such people must receive in themselves that recompense of their error which is meet because they do that which is against nature and the higher laws given by God.

Those who lack faith and character may be attracted to

almost any one of the opposite sex, and they may show no tendency to faithfulness to any one. There can not be trust of one another because each knows too much about the other. This is a sad state of affairs, and there can be no hope of a happy marriage when there cannot be proper trust and confidence. Parents, preachers, teachers, and all others who have a part in the training of young people need to help them understand that they are more than animals. God has given them great potential for true love, but they are also capable of degradation and vulgarity. They need to guard their lives very carefully lest they turn aside from the holy to the unholy.

An overmuch display of affection is not only an invitation to sin, but it is also very distasteful to the people who see it. A couple can win criticism and lose friends by forgetting that they are not alone in the world but that others are seeing their behavior. They may be so much in love that they can scarcely speak to others in a public gathering but must huddle in the least possible amount of space to fondle and caress one another and to whisper sweet nothings into each other's ears. The two may be morally clean and pure, but they leave room for questions in the minds of those who see them. Discretion is always in order. They will win praise and respect if they can conduct themselves properly during this period of courtship.

This excessive fondling and petting that is so often seen in couples who are in love has great danger attached to it. The sex instinct is stimulated and aroused to such a degree that two young people who had planned to remain pure for the wedding day may reach the point of no return, and fornication may result which will make its scar on their souls and consciences for life. Why play with fire, young man and young woman? Do you not have any common interests to employ your time so that you have nothing to talk about and nothing to do? A couple should first be very good friends before they fall in love. Too often the couple who has made a public display of affection before marriage soon find after marriage that the physical attraction was the only thing they had in common, and they have nothing on which to build a lasting relationship. Restraint of physical feelings and a cultivation of the proper interests which they share could prove to be a mark of wisdom. Neighbors who see them as they display their feelings so openly may well suppose that they use no restraint whatever in private. This may not be true, but it is easy to see why those who look on would think so, and the young couple should have no hard feelings toward those who judge them by their public actions. A lack of discretion can do much harm to a good name and can open the door to the soul destroying sin of fornication. Remember the short sentence in 1 Cor. 6:18: "Flee fornication." Do not invite it.

Even in times of worship when the church has assembled, a couple may win the disgust of their friends by their utter lack of consciousness that there are others in the room with them. They may hold hands, smile, whisper, and even embrace while the songs are being sung, prayers are being uttered, and even while the Lord's Supper is being observed. It is evident that it is not a period of worship for them. Preachers have often tried to speak to a couple concerning these matters, and they have learned to expect sharp, angry, and bitter reviling from the mothers. It is much more often that the mothers will show an ugly attitude than that the couple will. The couple knows full well that the preacher is in order when he speaks to warn, but a mother usually feels that he is out of place. If she allows such conduct on the part of her son or daughter without rebuking him or her, she feels that no one else has any right to interfere. The young couple can often take the rebuke from the preacher and profit from it because each may realize that he or she is flirting with sin. The violent reaction of the mothers may be at least a subconscious realization of their own guilt of neglect of parental duty.

I have heard Homer Hailey, whom I regard as a very godly man, lecture before young people and adults on the Old Testament book of "Song of Solomon." He views the book as a poetic portrayal of mating love. I believe he is right in so doing. The Bible touches on every phase of a man's life, and I believe we are given in the book a beautiful song of true love. The lovely rustic maiden longed for her shepherd lover, preferring his love to all the wealth and beauty that could surround her if she accepted the proffered love of the king. There is only beauty and loveliness in the picture of two young people who love one another in the way the Lord intended. It is so very sad that in our day singers and actors have misused the word love and turned it into a sordid picture of lust and sin. They do not know the beauty of holiness or the corruption of ungodliness.

Part of the preparation for marriage is the preparation for a period of courtship which is beautiful to all and absolutely above reproach. Discretion is a part of wisdom.

When you are planning your marriage, young man, ask yourself the question: Do my parents and most worthy friends consider it a good marriage, or do they think that I am making a mistake? You would be very wise to listen to what they have to tell you because they are probably right. Test your marriage plans in the light of your own power to reason, and do not ignore the counsel of those who know you best and love you most. A wise plan looks best in the open light. When many lights along the road of life are yellow or red, one should not rush ahead at full speed with foolish disregard for the danger signs. Ask yourself: Would the Lord approve my plans? Would He be pleased with the mate I have chosen? Are you able to know His mind and take His counsel?

Every failure in marriage brings sorrow and shame to the partners in the marriage, to the children in the home, and to all friends and loved ones who see the breakdown of another home. Knowing the seriousness of a failure should make one more careful in his choice of a companion and in his determination to do all in his power to succeed.

Parents, teachers, preachers, and all others should do their very best to help young people cultivate the character, knowledge, and wisdom that will prepare them for marriage. These same friends should warn them of and try to shield them from the dangers that face them in their period of preparation. Let all who know the word of God teach it diligently to the young whenever there is an opportunity that all can have a part in building better homes in the future that God may be glorified and families blessed by the good homes that can be built even in a wicked world.

Chapter 3

THE MAN'S PLACE

I have found much to strengthen my faith in God in the fact that the Bible is so complete in every detail. It instructs a man concerning his duties as a son, a husband, a father, a citizen of his government, a neighbor in his community, and even in his treatment of his enemy. It instructs him concerning his duty to God, to his brethren in Christ, and to the elders who are over him in the church or to the flock if he himself is an elder. His duties are many, and his relationships are many. He cannot conduct himself so properly in one relationship that he can be excused from his duties and responsibilities in another relationship. He must be faithful in discharging his duty in every situation of life so that he may be a well-rounded person who will be pleasing in the sight of God.

We are interested just now in his place in the home. The key word for his duties there is the word "provide." He is to be a provider. "If any provide not for his own, and specially for those of his own house, he hath denied the faith, and is worse than an infidel." (1 Tim. 5:8.)

There are many things that must be provided. We often think of the necessities of life as being food, shelter, and clothing. These are essentials and without them a family would be in great need. These are the things which money can buy, and the man is to work that he may have sufficient money to provide them.

We live in a day when there are many able-bodied men who had rather beg than work. They had rather be supported by tax money than to hold jobs which would provide them with a living salary. I have no word of criticism for those who are handicapped in any way which makes them unable to work if they receive help from tax sources or in some other way. I am not now thinking of them. I am thinking of able-bodied men who have so little respect for themselves and their families that they will just sit down and allow somebody else to feed them. That is a disgrace. Paul found some such men in the church at Thessalonica. He called their behavior "walking disorderly." "Now we command you, brethren, in the name of our Lord Jesus Christ, that ye withdraw yourselves from every brother that walketh disorderly, and not after the tradition which he received of us. For yourselves know how ye ought to follow us: for we behaved not ourselves disorderly among you; neither did we eat any man's bread for nought; but wrought with labour and travail night and day, that we might not be chargeable to any of you: not because we have not power, but to make ourselves an ensample unto you to follow us. For even when we were with you, this we commanded you, that if any would not work, neither should he eat. For we hear that there are some which walk among you disorderly, working not at all, but are busybodies. Now them that are such we command and exhort by our Lord Jesus Christ, that with quietness they work, and eat their own bread." (2 Thess. 3:6-12.)

If there is some one in the church of our Lord today who had rather just sit down and rest and let somebody else bring everything to him, he should be considered as walking disorderly. A man is to work that he may eat his "own" bread, the bread that he has provided for himself.

A man is not even up to the level of the animals and the birds if he does not care for those of his own house, his own family. The animals and birds provide for their young. He has "denied the faith and is worse than an infidel." An infidel is an unbeliever, and "he that believeth not shall be damned." If an infidel is going to be damned, and if one who will not provide for his own is worse than an infidel, he is indeed in a sad plight. What will be his condition at the judgment?

Honest toil is not something for which one should be ashamed. The most menial task is honorable if it provides things honest in the sight of all men. A mother once asked me to talk to her teenaged daughter who, she felt, was ashamed to be seen doing common labor. It was in the days when cotton was chopped and picked by hand, and all members of the family had to pitch in and help with the work. This young teenager was a good worker in the house, and she was a good worker in the back of the field out of sight of neighbors and strangers who might pass along the road. She had the feeling that if she was out there in the field, dressed for work and perhaps dirty from the work, she was disgraced. We may feel a wave of sympathy for the girl because we can understand her feelings when she had friends in other financial circumstances who did not have to work as she did, yet she needed the lesson her mother was trying to teach her. Work is honorable, and no one should be embarrassed when she is seen working. None of us has much sympathy for the able-bodied man who will not work or is ashamed to be seek working. He should reverse the feeling and be ashamed to be seen doing nothing when it is time to work.

From the time that Adam and Eve were driven out of the garden until now, God has ordained that "in the sweat of thy face shalt thou eat bread, till thou return unto the ground; for out of it wast thou taken: for dust thou art, and unto dust shalt thou return." (Gen. 3:19.) God has not made things easy for man in this life. He has made it necessary that he have to work in order to live and in order for his family to live.

"But as touching brotherly love ye need not that I write unto you: for ye yourselves are taught of God to love one another. And indeed ye do it toward all the brethren which are in all Macedonia: but we beseech you, brethren, that ye increase more and more; and that ye study to be quiet, and to work with your own hands, as we commanded you; that ye may walk honestly toward them that are without, and that ye may have lack of nothing." (1 Thess. 4:9-12.)

The man is to work with his own hands so that he may be able to pay his honest debts and have lack of nothing. He is to study to be quiet. Perhaps that implies that he is not to go around whining and complaining about his lot in life but just to get busy and better his lot if he can. If not, then he needs to learn, as Paul said, "in whatsoever state I am therewith to be content." (Phil. 4:11.)

The Lord honored the working man. When He chose His apostles, He selected them from among the working class of people. Will Rogers once said that the Lord must love common people because He made so many of them. I will say that He evidently loves working people because

He made so many of them. We have an old proverb which
says, "An idle brain is the devil's workshop." That is very
true. There would be much less crime in our country today
if young people were taught how to work and had the
urgent need to work or starve. If any man will not work
then he should not be allowed to eat.

Now, there are two sides to every coin. On the one side,
some go to the one extreme of not working at all, and,
having no business of their own, they busy themselves in
the affairs of others and become parasites and idlers and a
disgrace to society. On the other side, there are some who
fall so in love with money and the things that money can
buy that they work themselves to death. They are never
content with what they have, and they neglect health,
family, and religion for money.

"Godliness with contentment is great gain. For we
brought nothing into this world, and it is certain that we
can carry nothing out. And having food and raiment let us
be therewith content. But they that will be rich fall into
temptation and a snare, and into many foolish and hurtful
lusts, which drown men in destruction and perdition. For
the love of money is the root of all evil: which while some
coveted after, they have erred from the faith, and pierced
themselves through with many sorrows. But thou, O man
of God, flee these things; and follow after righteousness,
godliness, faith, love, patience, meekness." (1 Tim.
6:6-11.)

Some want money so much that covetousness becomes
idolatry. You know, if I had a silver dollar I could hold it
so close to my eye that it could hide the sun from my
sight. If it gets too close to the eye, it blinds. The god of
this world can blind one to the spiritual values and treasures. There are those who are not content with what they
can earn with a reasonable amount of toil and a reasonable
amount of time, with their skill and talent. It is not a sin
for a man to have something laid up for the future, but for
him to fall so in love with money that it becomes his god is
a sin.

I remember a young man who went to school to me
many years ago who seldom saw his father. The father
went to work early in the morning before his son was
awake. He came home in the evenings when his son had
gone to bed. It was not that the company where he worked
demanded such long hours. When his eight hour job was

finished he went to another job which he was doing on the side so that he could make more money. He did not see his children, so he did not know that his early teenaged son had suddenly grown from a little boy to the height of a man. The sad part was that his clothes did not change sizes as he did, and he outgrew them with nobody to see that they needed replacing. His father was too busy working. His extra job was not taken because he could not make a living with the one eight hour job he already had. He was making what was considered a good living wage at the time. He took the extra job so that he could make more money. He was not providing for his family. He was making money. He not only neglected his family, he also forsook the Lord. On weekends he had more time to work on his second job and could make more money. When his son was ready for college he had to struggle to make his own way because his father seemingly barely knew of his existence much less of his needs. That is a very extreme case, I will admit, but I knew the family. It may have been good for the children in some ways to have to struggle to make ends meet, but it was a sad reflection on the man who made a vast amount of money and let his family suffer for the necessities of life. "The love of money is the root of all evil." Those who reach for it to such an extent as I have described "pierce themselves through with many sorrows" even in this life and must face God in the judgment to answer for their deeds. In the case of the man I have described, I think there was more to his problem than just the love of money. He had the sort of personality that made him shun people, even those of his own family. He used his work as an escape from reality. He was shunning the responsibilities of parenthood because he did not know how to face them. He was not prepared in any way for a normal home life. He was to be pitied, along with the feeling of scorn that most of us felt for him, because he was cutting himself off from pleasures and companionships that could have meant so much to him. He needed his wife and children as much as they needed a husband and father.

They are the two sides of the coin: the man who will not work and is worse than an infidel and the man who has made money his god and neglects everything of value in life in working to gain it.

A man is to provide the money that his family needs.

He is the head of the house, and it is his responsibility to see that the physical needs of the family are provided. God made him the head, and every member of the family should recognize his position. This position as head however is not a pedestal on which he sits from which he issues orders to servants under him. It is rather a position of leadership, and he is to lead in a direction which will be right for his family to follow. That means first of all that he is walking as God directs. He must be a Christian to be the kind of head the home needs. Christ provides proper leadership for His church, which is His bride. The man likewise is to provide proper leadership for his wife and love her as Christ also loved the church. Whereas the man is head of the wife, and she must recognize him as such, he makes her position easy and pleasant by loving her and providing for her. "For the husband is the head of the wife, even as Christ is the head of the church: and he is the saviour of the body. Therefore as the church is subject unto Christ, so let the wives be to their own husbands in every thing. Husbands, love your wives, even as Christ also loved the church, and gave himself for it." (Eph. 5:23-25.)

The man is to give honor to his wife as the weaker vessel and recognize her need for his protection. She is an heir with him in the grace of life and in the sight of God is his equal. (Gal. 3:28,29.) If he fails to treat her with the proper care and respect, God will not hear his prayers. (1 Pet. 3:7.) He owes her love and honor just as certainly as he owes her the physical necessities of life, and they are things that money cannot buy. Having a good wife with whom a man can share the intimacy of married life is the greatest protection a man has against the serious sin of fornication. (1 Cor. 7:1-6.) He is to render his wife due benevolence just as she does him, and he is to realize that she has power over his body just as he has over hers. The two of them can by showing due benevolence the one to the other make a home that will bring happiness to them and their children, be a blessing to the community, and be pleasing in the sight of God.

The woman was created for the man that she might be a suitable companion for him and to fill his need. She is part of his very nature, completing his nature. When the man realizes that she is an integral part of himself, he will treat her in the way God ordained. (Gen. 2:18.)

When a man becomes a father he takes on many added responsibilities beyond those he has toward his wife. He sustains a vastly different relationship to his children. He must provide their food, shelter, and clothing. These things they have a right to expect from him so long as they are unable to provide for themselves. A man who will not provide the necessities for his children without complaining and scolding does not deserve to have children. He should recognize their needs and conduct himself before them in such a way that they have no hesitancy in asking him for the things that money can buy. He should be one who can be easily and pleasantly approached. These are things that they have every right to expect from their father, and he should provide generously and pleasantly in keeping with his ability.

There are two sides to this coin also. There are men with financial ability who will not provide for their children because they are not interested in their welfare. They do not see their needs and have no communication with them. They do not encourage their children to talk with them, so they do not know when they need clothes, school supplies, or other things. They ignore and neglect them. If they are made aware of the needs they are not willing to provide them because they have other plans for their money. Even though there may be money in the bank which could be used for the needs, it could also be used for something that would give the father selfish pleasure. Selfishness is a very sad characteristic of some fathers and is more common than we may realize. They may put their own interests and desires above the needs of the family.

There is the other side of the coin. There are fathers who pamper and coddle their children, never denying them anything for which they ask. There are more toys than they can possibly play with, more trips than they can enjoy, more games than they can play. They thus teach their children to make more and more requests. Anything they see that another child owns, anything they see advertised on television, anything they see displayed in stores, they must have; and so a generation of unrestrained, selfish children is produced. This attitude on the part of the father is often a result of what he thinks of as privation in his own childhood. He wants his children to have all the things that he missed as a child, and he tries to gain satisfaction for himself in giving them more than they need or

can enjoy. He destroys their imagination and their inge-
nuity in improvising the things which they do not have
and which would develop skills and talents for their future
usefulness. The children grow up supposing that whatever
they desire can be had simply by asking for it, and if it is
not quickly forthcoming they may learn to steal and beg
for it instead of working to supply it honestly.

In the last few decades there has been a rise in juvenile
crimes, due partly to the fact that teenagers have grown
up thinking they should never be denied anything.

In the city of Miami there is a large population of Cuban
refugees, who have fled their native Cuba to escape the
tyranny of a dictator. They had been taught to work hard
for everything they had, and most of them have done well
in the States. Just now, however, according to a report in
the *U. S. News and World Report* of April 5, 1976, crime
is on the rise among their young people. A spokesman for
the Dade County police department reported: "Cuban juvenile crime initially was almost negligible, because of the
very strong family structure. Unfortunately, as the parents have become more Americanized and the children are
allowed more freedom, juvenile crime has, in fact, increased. That's one part of our culture that we wish they
could avoid."

To sum up the two sides of the coin, we may say that a
man should provide the necessities and even luxuries
within reason for his children while at the same time re-
straining them from excessive spending and thinking that
the world owes them a living. He is not to indulge them in
every frivolous desire and give them the feeling that they
must never be denied anything which strikes their fancy.

The father owes much more to his children than the
physical necessities of life. There are many things that
money cannot buy which are necessary for children to
grow up to be normal, well developed men and women. He
must provide leadership, guidance, and example for them.
He must be one to whom they can look for advice and
counsel. He teaches many good things just by his worthy
example. On the other hand, if he is not going in the right
direction himself, he teaches the wrong things by his example. He must guide, direct, and train them. "And, ye
fathers, provoke not your children to wrath: but bring
them up in the nurture and admonition of the Lord."
(Eph. 6:4.) Children are to be taught the whole counsel of

God. There is much that can be taught by example, and a child is not likely to listen very well to words spoken if the example he sees in his father is not in harmony with his words, but there must be much teaching by word of mouth also. The father may think since he brings in the money for the physical needs of the family that he is excused from the responsibility of teaching his children. He may leave that to his wife. She may work also, and her time at home may be spent in caring for the clothes, the food, and other such things. She may also be limited in time just to talk with the children. Who, then, is going to tell them the stories of Joseph, Daniel, David, Ruth, and Jesus? Who is going to see that they have studied their lessons for Sunday morning's class? The mother cannot be free from sharing the responsibility, but the first duty is placed on the father as the head of the family to "bring them up in the nurture and admonition of the Lord." How can he bring his children up in the nurture and admonition of the Lord if he does not know what that means, if he is not a Christian, and if he does not know what the Bible says? Every man should do some serious thinking before he becomes a father, because the very eternal destiny of his child's soul may be determined by his teaching or his failure to teach.

The father is to discipline his children. When we think of the word discipline we usually think of punishment, and it does carry that meaning, but it means far more than that. The first meaning that is given in the dictionary which I have open before me now (*Webster's Students Dictionary*) is "training which corrects, molds, strengthens, or perfects." Used as a verb, it means first "to develop by instruction and exercise, to train in self-control and obedience." The second meaning then is "to punish or chastise." A properly disciplined child is a happy child. The father must set certain guidelines for the child to follow, and as the child is carefully trained and molded to walk in those guidelines and to fit into the limitations set for him, he becomes a secure, well developed, obedient child who is able to control and restrain himself as he grows into manhood.

There are times when the child must be punished, and the father who fails to administer punishment when such is needed is failing in his God-given duty. He is also showing a lack of love for the child. I have heard a parent say, "I love him too much to punish him." The wise man of the Old Testament said, "He that spareth the rod hateth his son: but he that loveth him chasteneth him betimes." (Prov. 13:24.) He said also, "Chasten thy son while there is hope, and let not thy soul spare for his crying." (Prov. 19:18.) This implies that a child may be brought into proper subjection while he is young, but there may come a time, if correction is withheld, that all hope for his character is gone. The character a man has at forty may be determined to a great extent by the kind of training he had in the home before the age of twelve.

In speaking of the way God deals with His children the writer of Hebrews compares Him to an earthly father who chastens his son. He says, "My son, despise not thou the chastening of the Lord, nor faint when thou art rebuked of him: for whom the Lord loveth he chasteneth, and scourgeth every son whom he receiveth. If ye endure chastening, God dealeth with you as with sons; for what son is he whom the father chasteneth not? But if ye be without chastisement, whereof all are partakers, then are ye bastards, and not sons. ... Now no chastening for the present seemeth to be joyous, but grievous: nevertheless afterward it yieldeth the peaceable fruit of righteousness to them which are exercised thereby." (Heb. 12:5b-8,11.) A son who grows up without correction, without punishment, without restraint, without guidance, is like a child who has no father, but who is illegitimate.

A man cannot go one way and lead in another. His influence will follow the way he goes, and his children will not be deceived. Jesus said, "He that is not with me is against me; and he that gathereth not with me scattereth abroad." (Matt. 12:30.) If, therefore, a man is not actively teaching his children the whole counsel of God, he is leading them in the road to destruction.

A father is to teach his children obedience to their parents. The command to obey their parents is given directly to the children, and they become responsible for their own actions as soon as they are old enough to understand that responsibility, but they do not know it of themselves. They must be taught. "Train up a child in the way he should go: and when he is old, he will not depart from it." (Prov. 22:6.)

There are so many temptations that face the youth of our day that can be resisted only by those who have been drilled, trained, guided, and molded from babyhood in the principles of right and wrong. Again, it is the father's responsibility to see that they are taught properly. It takes time to teach, so one of the things that a father owes his children is time. We have already mentioned a father of my acquaintance who rarely saw his children and spent no time with them. Through the influence of a godly mother they may grow into good citizens and even good workers in the church, but it will not remove the guilt from the father's name, because the responsibility cannot be shifted. There should be time spent with the children just in talking about whatever interests them. When they are very small their interests are determined by the things they see in the home. As they reach school age their interests broaden, and it is a skilled parent who can keep himself aware of those interests. He should help them feel that anything that interests them is of interest to him also. They will have problems which arise which they need to discuss. The father should be the natural one to whom they could go. There would not be a generation gap if there were no communication gap. One of the most pleasant memories I have of my childhood is the talks my father and I had together. Some of the things that stand out were of so little significance, and yet for some reason I remember them all these years later. The things said may not have been very important, but the fact that he took time with me and talked with me as though I were important enough to share his interests was very important. The fact that he had time to walk with me through the woods and the fields, to make me a whistle, to talk about the crops, and discuss the affairs of the community still means a good deal to me after fifty years have passed.

There are many other things that a father owes his children which will be discussed under another chapter heading. We shall leave them for a later time. One of the most serious offenses a father can commit against his children is that of neglect. He owes them a proper portion of his time and his attention.

A man has responsibilities other than those to his wife and his children. "If any provide not for his own, and specially for those of his own house, he hath denied the faith, and is worse than an infidel." This indicates that there may be some for whom he is responsible who do not live at his house. He has duties as a son to his aged parents when they reach the time of ill health or infirmity when they cannot care for themselves. The command to "honor thy father and thy mother" is not given to children alone. No one ever reaches the time when it does not apply. One who shows dishonor to his parents is displeasing in the sight of the Lord. The wise man said, "Whoso curseth his father or his mother, his lamp shall be put out in obscure darkness." (Prov. 20:20.) In this day of federal, state, and local welfare care for the aged and infirm, the children may feel a lack of responsibility to care for their parents. With Social Security, insurance policies, and pensions there may be less need for money to be provided by the children, but there is always a need for love, attention, and other things that money cannot buy. Older people so very often suffer from loneliness, which the children have an obligation to relieve whenever it is possible. Unfortunately, a great many old people lose their sense of gratitude and thoughtfulness of others so that they become unwelcome burdens on their children, and the children are helpless to remedy the situation in pleasant ways. Yet they cannot shift their responsibilities to unfeeling institutions and feel relieved of all care.

There may sometimes be more distant relatives for whom a man is responsible, and whenever and wherever the need arises he should be ready and willing to do what he can in keeping with his ability.

The man has a great responsibility in the field of benevolence. He must be a good neighbor. Jesus said that the first commandment is to love God, and the second that is very closely akin to it is to love one's neighbor as himself. A man has not fulfilled his obligation to God or to his own family if he has not set the worthy example of reaching out his hand to help others beyond his own yard who may be in need.

In answering the question of a certain lawyer who asked, "Who is my neighbor?" Jesus gave a very beautiful parable which serves as an example to all today as we deal one with another. He said, "A certain man went down from Jerusalem to Jericho, and fell among thieves, who stripped him of his raiment, and wounded him, and departed, leaving him half dead. And by chance there came down a certain priest that way: and when he saw him, he passed by on the other side. And likewise a Levite, when he was at the place, came and looked on him, and passed by on the other side. But a certain Samaritan, as he journeyed, came where he was: and when he saw him, he had compassion on him, and went to him, and bound up his wounds, pouring in oil and wine, and set him on his own beast, and brought him to an inn, and took care of him. And on the morrow when he departed, he took out two pence, and gave them to the host, and said unto him, Take care of him; and whatsoever thou spendest more, when I come again, I will repay thee." (Luke 10:30-35.)

The Samaritan was not related to the man who fell among the thieves, neither did he live next door to him. Yet in some way he was his neighbor. He owed an obligation to him simply because he was in need, and he himself had the ability to relieve. One's ability coupled with one's opportunity becomes one's responsibility.

So, the work of a man has varied aspects, and the Bible deals with his every relationship. It is very difficult to fulfill one's obligation in every way, but in order to be pleasing in the sight of God he must do so to the very best of his ability. He will be richer for doing so because he will have the promise of the life that now is and of that which is to come.

Chapter 4

THE WOMAN'S PLACE

Eph 5:21-22

Woman has a very important place to fill. She has work to do in the home, in the community, and in the church. The Bible has much to say about her place.

In thinking of her work, it is very easy to prove by the scriptures that her place is one of quiet subjection. It is not a place of noisy prominence or display. In 1 Peter 3:1, we find these words, "Likewise, ye wives, be in subjection to your own husbands." We will not notice more of the passage just now but will return to it later. If the Bible suggests a thing, there is good reason for its being suggested. Women's Liberation Movements may rise and fall, but the Bible still says, "Ye wives, be in subjection to your own husbands." The Bible does not change with the changing of philosophy and the reasoning of psychologists. The Bible is right and has always been right.

"Wives, submit yourselves unto your own husbands, as unto the Lord. For the husband is the head of the wife, even as Christ is the head of the church: and he is the Saviour of the body. Therefore as the church is subject unto Christ, so let the wives be to their own husbands in everything." (Eph. 5:22-24.) Now, the husband is the head of the wife, and the wife is to be in subjection to her own husband. I do not have to wonder if that is appropriate or if it is out of date. It may not be in harmony with the thinking of some of the political figures of our day, but when Heaven speaks there is wisdom behind what is said.

The same idea is expressed in almost the same words in Colossians 3:18. "Wives, submit yourselves unto your own husbands, as it is fit in the Lord." I do not believe that the Lord is suggesting an unpleasant duty. I do not believe that the place of submission is an unpleasant place. In both Ephesians and Colossians, the advice to the wives is followed by the expression, "Husbands, love your wives." In the first passage we noticed we would have found advice to the husbands if we had read a little further. It tells the husbands to dwell with them in knowledge, giving honor to the wives, and it mentions in particular that they are heirs together of the grace of life. Before God there is neither male nor female, just as there is neither Jew nor Gentile, and there is neither bond nor free. If the wife is a true Christian she is an heir of God, just as is her husband who is a Christian. Therefore, they are heirs together of the grace of life. So, in the sight of God, the man and the woman are equal. In the relationships of this life he is her head, and she is subject to him.

In the home there must be somebody in charge. Every school needs a principal. Every business needs a manager. Every state needs a governor. Every nation needs a president, a prime minister, a king, or somebody in charge. There must in every condition be somebody at the head. There is a position of leadership required where there is any sort of partnership or organization that involves a number of people. Just so, the home must have a head. There are some great advantages in not being the head. I often think of the days when I tried to serve as the principal in some private school. There are many advantages in being a teacher off down the hall in a room with the children, shut away from the boy that needs to be disciplined, the irate mother who thinks Junior has been mistreated, and the teacher who does not like a certain school policy. I would shudder to think of having to undertake that great task of dealing with all the problems and having to worry over the bus situation and trying to keep peace among the faculty and student body now.

The wife is to be shielded from some of the blows that must fall in marriage. She is to be shielded from some of the decision making. She has another role to fill, and only she can fill it. In a jewelry store there is often a courteous saleslady at the front to serve customers. Back behind the scenes, shielded from the constant coming and going of the customers, is the well trained man who is able to take a watch apart and repair it. He has a very, very important work to do, but he is in the background. The wife is to be shielded from some of the problems in order that she may carry on her delicate work in the background. That does not imply that her work is not important.

I can prove from the scripture that woman's place is important, just as I can prove that it is a place of subjection. In the Old Testament we find this statement: "Whoso findeth a wife findeth a good thing, and obtaineth favor of the Lord." (Prov. 18:22.) In Genesis 2:18 we are told, "And the Lord God said, It is not good that the man should be alone; I will make him an help meet for him." The man needs a wife, and God created the woman to fill his need. God saw that it was not good for the man to be alone, so He created some one to be a helper for him who would be worthy of him and suggested: "For this cause shall a man leave his father and his mother and shall cleave unto his wife." (Gen. 2:24.) I have often likened woman's place to that of the motor of a car. It is very necessary to the functioning of the car, but it is under the hood and is not seen. Back of the great work that many men do are great wives who are quietly aiding and encouraging them. They are worthy helpers, and their work is very important.

What is a good woman worth? How would you measure the worth of a good wife or mother? The wise man did not attempt to tell us. He said her price is far above rubies. (Prov. 31:10.) He did not measure her value in coins or in precious stones. He said her price is "far above rubies." There is no way to measure it.

Looking again to the book of 1 Peter we can learn more about this quiet, submissive wife. "Likewise, ye wives, be in subjection to your own husbands; that, if any obey not the word, they also may without the word be won by the conversation of the wives; while they behold your chaste conversation coupled with fear. Whose adorning let it not be that outward adorning of plaiting the hair, and of wearing of gold, or of putting on of apparel; but let it be the hidden man of the heart, in that which is not corruptible, even the ornament of a meek and quiet spirit, which is in the sight of God of great price. For after this manner in the old time the holy women also, who trusted in God, adorned themselves, being in subjection to their own husbands: even as Sarah obeyed Abraham, calling him lord: whose daughters ye are, as long as ye do well, and are not afraid with any amazement." (1 Pet. 3:1-6.)

This good wife has adorned herself, not in clothes for the outward body that will attract attention and be gaudy and expensive, but rather in a meek and quiet spirit. Hers is an inner adorning which is in the sight of God of great price. While she is quiet, unassuming, and submissive, she is exercising an influence for good over her husband. If she has a husband who is not a Christian and who has not been touched by the word of God, he may yet be won when he sees the good example she sets before him. He may be won by her clean, pure, holy manner of life. She is not a nag. She lives her religion day by day before him, and he is caused to realize that there is truth in what she professes.

The woman is not to usurp authority over the man. (1 Tim. 2:12.) She is cheapening herself and her position when she seeks the limelight and tries to gain a prominent place on the social ladder or in the political arena with the man. She is getting out of her quiet place when she gets into the rough and tumble world of business and politics and seeks to gain prominence over the man. A man today would be less likely to tip his hat to a woman who has left her place. He would be less likely to get up in a crowded bus and give her a seat. She loses the respect of her husband when she usurps his position, and she loses the respect of other men as well. If a man gets up now on a crowded bus and gives a woman his seat, she may sit there and blow smoke in his face while he stands in the aisle trying to act the part of a gentleman. I have no doubt that he stands there wishing that he had his seat back. At least, the smoke from her cigarette might blow over his head if she were standing. If she is going to smoke like the men, and take up whatever other bad habits she can copy, she does not deserve any special respect. Why should a man tip his hat to a blaspheming, immoral reprobate that happens to be called a woman? Perhaps she does not want to be thought of as a woman. She is a person. She has lost her identity as a woman, and she has lost her quiet, lovely, meek, and holy place. It is the meek and quiet spirit that is honored by the Lord. The Lord does not put any emphasis on the fancy dress and special hairdo or on expensive jewelry. He looks on the heart.

When we say that the Lord does not put any emphasis on the outward appearance of a woman, I think we need to suggest that the very spirit of Christianity would demand that she be clean, neat, and attractive in her physical appearance. For her to be careless, untidy, and habitually sloven in her appearance would show a lack of respect for her husband. She had dressed before marriage in such a way as to gain his respect for her, and she should hold that respect by being as neat and attractive as she is able. This does not mean that she must spend a great deal of money in order to be attractive. That is not necessary. She needs to learn to use what she has in the best way possible. Cleanliness does not demand wealth. A poor woman with very few clothes can be clean and neat.

In 1 Timothy 2:9,10 Paul explains more about a woman's dress and demeanor. "In like manner also, that women adorn themselves in modest apparel, with shamefacedness and sobriety; not with broided hair, or gold, or pearls, or costly array; but (which becometh women professing godliness) with good works." The parenthetical expression "which becometh women professing godliness," explains the kind of thing He is recommending. The woman who professes to be godly will be modest. The word modest carries with it two ideas, both of which are important in the way a woman is to dress. It means "showing moderation, not excessive." This would imply that a woman's clothing should be neither expensive nor showy. It should be moderate in both details. The word means also "chaste, decent, virtuous." (Meanings taken from *Webster's Students Dictionary*.) She is not to dress in a way to attract attention because of the expense involved in the cost of her clothing. She is not to be dressed in far out, showy, gaudy clothing which will make her conspicuous in any setting. She is not to attract attention because her clothing shows a lack of chastity, decency, and morality.

There is another word in this passage which carries with it the idea which we usually mean when we say modest. It is "shamefacedness." It is "shamefastness" in the American Standard Version. From W. E. Vine's *An Expository Dictionary of New Testament Words* we have this meaning given: "A sense of shame, modesty, is used regarding the demeanour of women in the church. ... Shamefastness is that modesty which is 'fast' or rooted in the character." A woman who possesses the trait of shamefastness is shy, not bold; discreet, not puffed up with importance. She is modest. She must dress in such a way that she will not cause any comment that is indiscreet or in any way damaging to her character. The way she wears her hair, the kind and amount of jewelry she wears, and the emphasis she places on her clothing all denote the kind of character she possesses. She is to wear clothing that covers her body sufficiently so as not to incite lust or evil thoughts in the heart and mind of men who see her.

This woman who is properly dressed in the sight of God is clothed in quietness and meekness. Quietness is the exact opposite of loudness. In the seventh chapter of Proverbs we have a description of the strange woman, the harlot. She is said to be loud. That is not the same trait as quietness. It tells a great deal about her character. To be quiet does not mean that the good woman is never to open her mouth. In describing the virtuous woman in Proverbs 31 we are told, "She openeth her mouth with wisdom, and in her tongue is the law of kindness." (Prov. 31:26.) Not only is she to be quiet, but she is also to be meek. The word meek means "mild of temper, patient, longsuffering, humble." This carries with it the idea of not putting herself forward out of her place but maintaining her position of quiet importance with patience and without complaining.

The woman has duties besides those toward her husband. She is to be a good mother. "She shall be saved in child bearing, if they continue in faith and charity and holiness with sobriety." (1 Tim. 2:15.) There is more to being a mother than merely giving birth to children. "I will therefore that the younger women marry, bear children, guide the house, give none occasion to the adversary to speak reproachfully." (1 Tim. 5:14.) When the children are born, there begins a long, long period of caring for them. The mother's place is very important because the hand that rocks the cradle rules the world. It is a very great sphere where she can be saved in the quietness of her own home as she goes about her work of caring for her children.

We have mentioned elsewhere that every school needs a principal, every business needs a manager, every state needs a governor. There needs to be somebody in charge. Now, the husband is the head of the home, but much of the work of caring for the children is delegated to the wife, who is the mother. She is to "guide the house." That means that she is to keep things running smoothly. She must direct, guide, and train a man's most precious pos-

ildren. He goes off to work to earn the
his precious possessions in the hands of
he chose to be his companion and the
ren. She is to be faithful to the charge
itted to her.

ng women will not know how to conduct themselves
properly as wives and mothers if they are not taught. The
responsibility of teaching them is especially assigned to
aged women. After telling the behavior pattern that they
are to follow, the writer says, "That they may teach the
young women to be sober, to love their husbands, to love
their children, to be discreet, chaste, keepers at home,
good, obedient to their own husbands, that the word of
God be not blasphemed." (Tit. 2:4,5.) Which older woman
in our day teaches her daughter to love her husband and to
love her children? Do young women need to be taught
such? Does everybody just take for granted that women
will love their husbands and their children? They may not
do so unless they are well taught by word and example. I
believe there are many children born in America who are
not wanted. When they get here they are in the mother's
way. They tie her down, and she wants to go to the party,
or to the game, or to the river. She wants to run around
and be with the noisy crowd, and her little bundle that is
so precious is in her way. It annoys her. Aged women
should prepare young women as they grow up for the
responsibilities that they must face in the home. There
they can be queens. That is the place they are respected
most. That is the place heaven assigned them.

The woman is to love her husband and to love her children. She is to be a keeper at home. One of the things that
is wrong with young people in America today is that they
never did have mothers in the true sense of the word. They
have grown up in homes where there were no keepers.
When they came home from school there was nobody
there. There was nobody to share their triumphs or
sympathize in their troubles. They had nobody to care.
They were neglected, so they rebelled against everything
that stood for authority. Good mothers who were in their
proper places, doing the work God gave them to do, could
have done more to curb the riots and rebellions among the
youth a few years ago than all the police officers in the
whole nation. A home has something very seriously
lacking when there is no mother in it. America will never

turn back to God and to high moral integrity until somehow we can get keepers back into the homes who are sober, discreet, chaste, and adorned in the ornaments of a meek and quiet spirit. I want somebody somewhere to cry aloud in honor of motherhood. In times past there were many orations honoring the name of mother and the noble work she did in shaping the destiny of her children. In our day young women are taught and encouraged often by their own mothers to seek careers instead of home responsibilities. Marriage and motherhood are discredited so that many young women are choosing to remain unmarried and to avoid the ties and restrictions of motherhood.

The woman is not to teach or usurp authority over the man. (1 Tim. 2:12.) As we have seen, she has her own sphere of action and it is in no way to take prominence over the man. The elders in the church are to be men. The woman is not to have a place of prominence or authority in the church. Again, her place is one of quietness and submission. "Let your women keep silence in the churches: for it is not permitted unto them to speak; but they are commanded to be under obedience, as also saith the law. And if they will learn anything, let them ask their husbands at home: for it is a shame for a woman to speak in the church." (1 Cor. 14:34,35.) It is a shame and a disgrace and a rejection of the word of God when a woman pushes herself into a place of leadership in the church or in any way usurps the authority of the man.

When I was still a college student and quite young, I met a young man who was preaching for the Christian Church in the general area of the place where I was preaching. We each had a long distance to drive each weekend, so he suggested that we go together and share the cost. This we did one weekend, but we did not find the trip too pleasant. We found much more on which we disagreed in religious matters than on which we agreed. During the course of the trip, he told me that the church for which he was preaching was planning to appoint some new elders. He said, "I am determined to get some women on the board of elders. You know that women are inclined to be more religious than men. They will put more zeal into their work." I pointed out to him that the Bible says that the elder is to be the "husband of one wife." A woman cannot meet the qualifications. He was not much impressed because it concerned him little what the Bible said. Human reasoning was more important to him, but he admitted that there were some in the church who opposed the idea. We can be glad that there were a few who had one point straight, if their objections were based on their knowledge of the Bible.

A woman may get out of her place in other ways in the church. She may make decisions for the group, and this is particularly true in young, small churches where there is a shortage of leadership. She may, in her zeal to promote the work, step out of a meek, quiet place into prominence in dealing with matters of business, choosing a preacher, and directing affairs which are not becoming to her. I have seen new churches torn and practically destroyed by some woman who wanted so much to see it grow, but she caused trouble by getting out of her place. I am not always wise in dealing with such situations, but I know that the Bible says she is not "to usurp authority over the man." She is not to be the elder, and she is not to act like one. She is not to speak in a public authoritative way in handling the business affairs of the church.

While a woman cannot take the public place in the church and in any way usurp authority over the man, she yet has a very important place to fill in the field of teaching. "The aged women likewise, that they be in behavior as becometh holiness, not false accusers, not given to much wine, teachers of good things; that they may teach the young women to be sober, to love their husbands, to love their children, to be discreet, chaste, keepers at home, good, obedient to their own husbands, that the word of God be not blasphemed." (Titus 2:3-5.) This is a very important place of teaching, and we have already had occasion to refer to it as we noticed her work of training young women for their roles as wives and mothers. She is to teach her own children. Timothy was trained by a godly mother and a devout grandmother. Paul, in speaking of him, was filled with joy when he remembered "the unfeigned faith that is in thee, which dwelt first in thy grandmother Lois, and thy mother Eunice; and I am persuaded that is in thee also." From a child Timothy had known the holy scriptures. He was greatly blessed by having the good mother and the good grandmother to instruct him early in the scriptures. There would likely not have been such a young man as Timothy without the women to teach him. He became a partner with Paul in the

great work of preaching the gospel. There co
Timothys now if there were more women like
Lois. They had "unfeigned faith," the gen\
which they could pass on to their children. That is
great work indeed that can be done right in the home.

There is an example recorded in the eighteenth chapter
of Acts of a woman who joined with her husband in teaching a man in a private manner. Apollos came to Ephesus
and began to preach. He was an eloquent man and mighty
in the scriptures, yet there were some things he did not
know. When Aquila and his wife Priscilla heard him they
recognized one with great ability and zeal and one who
would respond to further truth when he learned it; so
"they took him unto them, and expounded unto him the
way of God more perfectly." Priscilla was not out of place
in what she did. She is mentioned very favorably in other
passages to indicate that she was a worthy woman. There
are ways in which a woman may teach a man by word as
well as by example. She is always to do so with meekness
and respect. I believe I have learned many things from my
wife. I think she has recognized me as being responsible
for leadership in the home and as being her head, but I
have no reason not to learn from her. I have been a poor
student of some things, but she has sought to do her work
well. I know that my work would have been far less effective if she had not helped.

I want to honor woman as a teacher. She can and must
teach her children. She must teach young women, not only
her own daughters, but other women with whom she
comes in contact. She can teach her neighbors. She often
has an opportunity with her neighbor women that a
preacher cannot have. She meets them socially. They
borrow from and lend to one another. She can gain their
respect by her chaste behavior, and she can set a good example before them which can lead to an opportunity to
teach the word of God. Even the very old woman can have
opportunities for this good example and words of wisdom
if she will exercise her proper abilities. Too often as one
grows old she grows bitter and cynical, feeling that she is
being abused and neglected. She becomes a false accuser,
as Titus warned against. Her head hurts, her back aches,
her strength is gone, old friends die, and she is left to
whine and bemoan her lot in life. If she has lived a good,
rich life in the service of the Lord and has gained knowl-

edge and wisdom through the years she can make younger
friends when those her age are gone. She could make her
one room a gathering place for young people who would
seek her company because "she openeth her mouth with
wisdom; and in her mouth is the law of kindness." (Prov.
31:26.) Growing old need not be a burden to the one who
grows old or to those who care for her, if she has developed
the good disposition, the love for truth, and an interest in
other people that she should. Her life can continue to bless
and instruct others whom she meets.

We have already mentioned that a woman has the obligation to teach her neighbors when she has opportunity.
In the field of benevolence she has a duty to them also.
She must show herself willing to help in whatever capacity
she is able to serve. When there is sickness, she is to provide care if she is able to do so. She may be needed to care
for the children of a sick neighbor. There may be food
needed. The house may need cleaning. No task should be
too lowly for her to do when there is great need. "The poor
ye have always with you," Jesus said; so there will come
at various times occasions when she can and must provide
for the poor. The virtuous woman described in Proverbs
31 set an example for all women to follow. "She stretcheth
out her hands to the poor; yea, she reacheth forth her
hands to the needy." (v. 20.)

Often a woman is left a widow when she is still in good
health. Her family has grown to adulthood, and she is left
alone without the care of a household. Many such women
obtain gainful employment because they are forced by circumstances to support themselves or to supplement their
support. There are others who do not need the extra
money necessarily but work in order to be busy because
they can be more contented that way. Then there are some
who do not need to work to support themselves and seemingly are not looking for something to do in order to make
life meaningful again. They merely sit down to bemoan
their fate. They waste many valuable hours that could be
devoted to visits to the sick and needy where just their
presence could relieve loneliness and add enjoyment to
another life. I believe there are too many wasted widow-
hours. Too many have depended on their husbands and
children for companionship and have built their lives
completely around their home duties so that they are lost
and desolate without them. We are not trying in any way

to minimize their loss and grief, but we are suggesting that they might be able to relieve their own needs by supplying help to others. Every woman has something that she can contribute to the good of others if she will recognize the fact and apply herself diligently in meeting the challenge.

In the New Testament we have a brief story of just the kind of woman that I am trying to recommend to all in our day. It is such a beautiful little story and provides such a wonderful example of what one woman can do in service to others that I would like to notice the entire account. "Now there was at Joppa a certain disciple named Tabitha, which by interpretation is called Dorcas: this woman was full of good works and almsdeeds which she did. And it came to pass in those days, that she was sick, and died: whom when they had washed, they laid her in an upper chamber. And forasmuch as Lydda was nigh to Joppa, and the disciples had heard that Peter was there, they sent unto him two men, desiring him that he would not delay to come to them. Then Peter arose and went with them. When he was come, they brought him into the upper chamber: and all the widows stood by him weeping, and showing the coats and garments which Dorcas made, while she was with them. But Peter put them all forth, and kneeled down, and prayed; and turning him to the body said, Tabitha, arise. And she opened her eyes: and when she saw Peter, she sat up. And he gave her his hand, and lifted her up, and when he had called the saints and widows, presented her alive. And it was known throughout all Joppa; and many believed in the Lord." (Acts 9:36-42.) Dorcas made "coats and garments." In those days I suppose she may have made the thread and then the cloth and after that the garment. The great cost to her was the labor, but she had used her time and energy to make the things that the widows needed. There is so much to be done which involves very little money but which demands much time and concern. This willingness to show benevolence would break down much prejudice among one's neighbors and win respect for the one who shows it so that her word would carry great weight when she speaks.

Godly women may do much in the field of benevolence as did Dorcas. Some have more time than others to devote to such work, as we have mentioned in the case of able-bodied, unemployed widows; but all have some time that can be given to visiting the sick, the lonely, and the faint-hearted. One class of people that must not be overlooked when there is time to visit are the babes in Christ or those who have grown weary in their service to the Lord. Many have great discouragement at home and find it difficult to attend all the services, so they may allow themselves gradually to lose interest and drop out. They need encouragement. Telephone calls and home visits can mean very much to them because they are reminded that they have "brothers and sisters" in Christ who are concerned for their spiritual welfare. Women are especially fitted for this type of work because they can share the feelings of others more readily than men usually.

Among the very precious things that women can do is to give moral support to those, especially young men, who are preaching the gospel. It is not hard for me to remember the names of some faithful women who forty-five years ago gave me handshakes and words of encouragement when I was making my first feeble efforts to preach. Their words made me feel that they cared for me, and they made me work harder to do my best work. I am sure there are many good women who are interested in the truth and in those who are proclaiming it who do not express their feelings in words; but I would like to encourage them to do so because of the help to others. When there are problems that arise in the church, and preachers, elders, and others are being tested and driven almost to despair, the words of worthy women can help them to stand when they might be ready to fall. We cannot overestimate the powerful influence of godly women as they, in their quiet, humble place, stand behind those who need encouragement and strength in the fight for truth.

One of the great preachers during the period when the apostles lived was named Joses, but the apostles renamed him Barnabas, which means Son of Consolation. I have known many women who might well be renamed Daughters of Consolation because of the spirit they manifested toward others.

A woman cannot be such a good wife that she need not be a good mother. She cannot be such a good mother that she need not be a good wife. She has strict duties to both her husband and her children, and she must not neglect either. She cannot be such a good keeper at home that she fails to see her duty to her neighbors. Most important of all: she cannot serve her husband, children, and community so well that she can be excused from serving God. She cannot serve faithfully in any capacity whatever if first she is not serving God. He created her and gave her the abilities which she possesses, so her first allegiance is to Him and then to her family and her community. The same instructions that are given to the man for his obedience to God are also given to the woman. She is to be a faithful Christian. It is the man who is assigned the public work in the church, but there in the pews are women who are just as faithful and acceptable to God as they worship regularly as He has ordained.

Paul summed up the qualities of a good woman when he wrote to Timothy concerning a widow who might be cared for by the church, who having been the wife of one man was to be "well reported of for good works; if she have brought up children, if she have lodged strangers, if she have washed the saints' feet, if she have relieved the afflicted, if she have diligently followed every good work." (1 Tim. 5:9,10.)

Chapter 5

THE CHILD'S PLACE

"Lo, children are an heritage of the Lord: and the fruit of the womb are his reward. As arrows are in the hand of a mighty man; so are children of the youth. Happy is the man that hath his quiver full of them: they shall not be ashamed, but they shall speak with the enemies in the gate." (Ps. 127:3-5.)

One of the greatest blessings that the Lord pronounced upon the faithful of the Old Testament was the promise of many children. To Abraham He promised, "That in blessing I will bless thee, and in multiplying I will multiply thy seed as the stars of the heaven, and as the sand which is upon the sea shore; and thy seed shall possess the gate of his enemies; and in thy seed shall all the nations of the earth be blessed; because thou hast obeyed my voice." (Gen. 22:17,18.)

When Rebekah was leaving her father's house in Haran to go to the land of Canaan to become Isaac's wife, her family said to her, "Be thou the mother of thousands of millions, and let thy seed possess the gate of those which hate them." (Gen. 24:60.)

Children are intended by the Lord to be a great blessing to their parents. They are a heritage of the Lord, a gift passed down from Him to be preserved and used in a way to benefit the home and all others around. In the society in which we live, there are many people who do not look upon children as a blessing but rather, if not quite a curse, at least a hindrance to them. They are unwilling to accept the responsibilities that come with them, so the children are unwanted before birth and unloved afterwards. The Lord

66

did not so intend. He intended that they should bless the family and increase the very purpose for being alive. They should give the parents a challenge, and they should be precious to them.

The psalmist said that they are as arrows in the hands of a mighty man. This is the picture of a hunter as he goes out to seek game. Arrows are his weapons to obtain his food supply. Children are a man's help in providing the stimulus for him to work as God ordained that he should. They are his aspirations for reaching his goals in life. They provide pleasure and love along the way. A man has no pleasure in life that can equal the joy that he can have in his children. Their talk, their ways, their innocence, their dependence are a perpetual interest and delight to him.

Arrows are also the hunter's defense against his enemies in the forest around him. One cannot go calmly straight ahead stalking his prey without always being watchful of the dangers that lurk all around him. Just so, in life as a man pursues his goals he must keep constant watch for those things that can destroy him and what he is seeking. If he has children while he is young, they grow to adulthood at a time when he may need protection from poverty and want. They help in the battle of life. They are his security, his life insurance policy. How sad it is to see one grow old and infirm and have to be cared for by strangers. Children provide the care and attention that strangers cannot give in the same way. "Happy is the man that hath his quiver full of them." The future looks safe and happy to the one who has a family of good, well-behaved, obedient children. They are a surer, safer fortune laid up for their parents than any stocks or bonds could provide.

We are assuming in what we are saying that the children have the character that they should possess. Otherwise, if they grow up to be willful, stubborn, and ungrateful, they are certainly a man's weakness and not his strength. They become a curse rather than a blessing.

Arrows must be carefully formed and shaped so that they can be shot straight from the bow. Children must also be molded and shaped into the form that can prove a blessing to the parents. This shaping of a personality is one of the greatest responsibilities a parent has, and the character of a child is determined by the success one makes. The arrow will not hit its target if it is bent or

warped. Neither will the child reach that goal which will be
the end of his parents' dreams for him if he is not straight
and true. The arrow cannot hit its mark without the bow-
man's taking careful aim. The child cannot reach the mark
set for him without the careful planning and aim of the
parent.

Just as the Bible recommends that a young woman
marry, so also it recommends that she have children. "I
will therefore that the younger women marry, bear children, guide the house, give none occasion to the adversary
to speak reproachfully." (1 Tim. 5:14.) It is an unnatural
situation when a young lady does not desire to be a wife
and mother. Now, I do not believe that Paul was saying
that she must have children in order to go to heaven when
he said, "Notwithstanding she shall be saved in childbearing." (1 Tim. 2:15.) Rather he is saying that she can be
saved by performing the task assigned to her in the home,
and the idea of childbearing carries with it more than giving birth to a child. There is the life of caring for and training children that the birth necessitates. She should desire
this domestic life of child rearing because it gives her the
promise of joy and happiness as she sees her ideals unfold
in their lives.

It is amazing to me that there could be any one who
claims to be an atheist in our world. How could any one
look into the face of a newborn baby and doubt that there
is a God? There is the coloring, the very features of his
parents. He shows his very heritage in his face. It is said
of Seth that Adam begat a child in his own image. The
marvel of procreation is just as wonderful as the marvel of
creation. That a man can pass on to his child his very physical appearance is enough to make one believe that there
is a God back of the law of procreation. When the child is
born he has all the potential of becoming whatever those
in charge of his care and training desire for him.

In the very beginning God set in force the law of nature,
saying, "Let the earth bring forth grass, the herb yielding
seed, and the fruit tree yielding fruit after his kind, whose
seed is in itself, upon the earth: and it was so. And the
earth brought forth grass, and herbs yielding seed after
his kind, and the tree yielding fruit, whose seed was in itself, after his kind: and God saw that it was good. ... And
God said, Let the earth bring forth the living creature
after his kind, cattle, and creeping thing, and the beast of

the earth after his kind: and it was so. And God made the beast of the earth after his kind, and cattle after their kind, and every thing that creepeth upon the earth after his kind: and God saw that it was good." (Gen. 1:11,12,24,25.) Then God made man in His own image and decreed that man should bring forth after his kind. He said, "Be fruitful, and multiply, and replenish the earth." (v. 28a.) The law of nature still holds true. It is a wonderful thing to think that one generation can be followed by another, and that there can still be children born. They are God's gift to man.

One of the things that aged women are to teach the younger women is to love their children. (Tit. 2:4.) To love a child is to do for him whatever God has ordained to be done for him. We have both sides of the picture, looking at the command from the viewpoint of the child and the parents, when we read, "Children, obey your parents in the Lord: for this is right. Honour thy father and mother; which is the first commandment with promise; that it may be well with thee, and thou mayest live long on the earth. And, ye fathers, provoke not your children to wrath: but bring them up in the nurture and admonition of the Lord." (Eph. 6:1-4.)

Children, when very young, should be taught to say from memory, "Children, obey your parents in the Lord: for this is right." They should repeat it often so that when they are old enough to appreciate its meaning it will already be a part of their lives. Their place in the home is a place of subjection. They come into the world with no knowledge of right and wrong, of good and evil. They must look to parents to guide them in every word they say and in every act they perform. They must have strict guidance from the very first moment of their lives. They have no wisdom and no foresight, so they cannot determine their own way. "A child left to himself bringeth his mother to shame." (Prov. 29:15.) It is naturally the responsibility of the parents to teach the young child to be obedient, and when he has reached the age of understanding he is responsible for his own actions. He must then bear his own responsibility in being obedient to his parents.

"Children, obey your parents in all things: for this is well pleasing unto the Lord." (Col. 3:20.) I want to emphasize the word "all." It is easy enough for a child who is old enough to have ideas of his own to obey his parents when they suggest the things that he wants to do. It is an entirely different matter when they suggest things that are contrary to his desires. That is the time when the true spirit of obedience can be seen. The Bible says that he is to obey in "all things," whether it pleases him or not. Why should he obey? It is enough that the parents have told him to do a thing. A good answer to him if he stops to question is just "Because I said so." I think that is the way my father would have answered me. Now, there are many times when the parent needs to give reasons and explain carefully why the child is being refused a request. Explanations and discussions are very much in order, and there should be the proper relationship between parent and child that will allow free expressions on the part of both. Each should feel no hesitancy in stating his reasons pro and con, and each should respect the feelings of the other; but when all is said and done, the final decision belongs to the parent. His son, because he is his son, must yield to his decision. I have no way of knowing what percentage of the children in our nation have that kind of attitude toward their parents. How many have learned that lesson? That is true obedience. It yields peaceable results. This is one of the finest ways I know of honoring parents and of showing proper respect.

It is not necessary for each new generation to make every mistake that the generations before have made. It is not necessary that each child make all the mistakes that his parents have made. He should be shielded from some of the mistakes simply because his parents have made them and have profited from them and now are trying to prevent his repeating them. The place of the child then is that of a pupil. He will learn not only from the things he hears in the home but also from the things he sees. If the parents are still making grievous mistakes before him, he will follow in their steps. If they have corrected their mistakes and are setting good examples before him, he will follow in that way also.

Children go through various phases in their attitude toward their parents. I remember a speech which the superintendent of schools made to my class when I was just a youngster. He said that a four year old child would defend his father against all odds even if that father were a reprobate. In the eyes of that four year old he could do no wrong. By the time the four year old has reached the teen-age he may wonder how parents as old-fashioned and ignorant as his could have such a bright, intelligent son. Now, I am quite sure that most children do not put the thought into words like that, but it may often be in their minds, and they may rather turn away in disgust at their parents' stupidity. They may wonder how their parents can be so ignorant that they cannot see the wisdom of this or that idea of their children. The superintendent said that after a while the son will change in his attitude, and then he may say, "Dad, how would you do this?" He may wonder how his father has suddenly gained so· much knowledge, and he feels the need of his advice and counsel. Some time later when he has grown older and faced many of the experiences that he did not know would come and has been baffled and discouraged by the problems he has met with his own children, he may look at his aging father and say, "Dad, how did you do it?" He may stand in amazement at the wisdom that his father has and wonder if he himself will ever know as much. It is unfortunate that children ever go through the period of thinking that their parents are old-fashioned and ignorant, but if the truth were told, I suspect most children do at some time or other have such a passing thought, at least.

In thinking of obedience, I would like to make the obser-vation that by the time a child reaches the age of account-ability he knows beyond much doubt what his father would say in almost every situation that arises whether the father is present or not. By then he has had access to his father's advice so long that he knows what things are acceptable and what are unacceptable. My father has been dead nearly thirty years, and my memory is not very good, but I think I could very well word his answer to any sensible, practical question I could ask. I lived in his house from my birth until I finished college. We were close and talked of many things during those years. I knew his spirit and his attitude. I can have the benefit today, nearly thirty years after his death, of his advice and counsel be-cause I knew the man well enough to know what he would suggest. I believe that any son who is old enough to go off on his own without his parents can still obey them in whatever situation arises, because he knows what they would say if he could ask their advice at that very moment.

In thinking of a child's knowing the spirit of his parents well enough to obey them even when absent from them, I am reminded of an expression in the New Testament that implies that we should know the Christ that well so that in all circumstances we, as His children, should obey Him. We are told, "Now if any man have not the Spirit of Christ, he is none of his." (Rom. 8:9b.) If we have learned enough of the Spirit of Christ from reading the story of His life in Matthew, Mark, Luke, and John and have seen how His principles and commands are carried out by a study of the epistles, then we should be able to know His answers to the problems we face day by day. We can learn much about what He said and did in various situations, and we can read how He answered the numerous questions that were asked Him, so that we can pretty well obey Him in every detail of life. Does He not say that that is exactly what we are to do? "And whatsoever ye do in word or deed, do all in the name of the Lord Jesus, giving thanks to God and the Father by him." (Col. 3:17.)

Let us apply that same principle to the instructions we are giving to our young people and modify the verse to read, "Whatsoever you do, at home, at work, at play, or wherever you are, do the will of your parents, young people." I do not believe that we have violated any rule of God in making the new verse, but rather we have explained the rule. That is genuine obedience. When you, young people, have reached the point when you respect and honor your parents for the wisdom they have gained in going those extra two or three decades down the road of life, you will have come a long way in learning to obey as you should.

Sometimes young people forsake the counsel of their parents and the counsel of other adults who have had many more years to observe the end to which various kinds of behavior lead. They may decide that they and their contemporaries have a monopoly on wisdom. In such cases the wise young people are headed for trouble. I am reminded of the young man Rehoboam who became king in the place of his father Solomon. He had the wisest man who ever lived for a father, and he should have gained knowledge and wisdom from both his good examples and his bad. He should also have profited from the wisdom of the old men who had been counselors to his father. Not so. He forsook their counsel and turned rather to those young men who had grown up with him. In thus doing, he plunged the entire kingdom into chaos and brought about a division that was never repaired as long as the two kingdoms that were formed remained.

By virtue of the fact that parents are older than their children, they should be in a position to command their respect and obedience. That is reason enough for the children to obey and honor them. Then there is the special reason that the Lord commanded it. There is an added reason, however, "That it may be well with thee, and thou mayest live long on the earth." The average life span of respectful, courteous, obedient young people is longer than that of the thoughtless and disobedient youths. The drug addicts, the slaves to alcohol, those given to dissipation of other types, breakers of speed laws, rebels against civil authority, and such like are not likely to have long lives. This is not meant to imply that no good child dies young or that no rebellious child lives to old age, but we are thinking of average conditions. A rebellious son brings many troubles on himself that the obedient son escapes.

We will discuss in another chapter the thought that it is the responsibility of the parent to teach and enforce the Lord's command that the child obey. Sufficient here to say that it is the duty of the child to obey. He must obey willingly and pleasantly. A child who does not obey willingly is a rebellious child. A child must learn to listen to his father's instructions that he may gain wisdom and accept the correction that he may gain mastery over himself. The wise man Solomon said, "A wise son heareth his father's instruction. ... A fool despiseth his father's instruction: but he that regardeth reproof is prudent. ... Correction is grievous to him that forsaketh the way: and he that hateth reproof shall die." (Prov. 13:1a; 15:1,10.) If a child is foolish and rebellious, it is a reflection on him if he is old enough to account for his actions. Regardless of his age, it is a reflection on his father, because the father has the duty of training him in his actions.

We hear a great deal today about a generation gap and a new breed of human beings that are called "teenagers." Has no other generation had teenagers? We have at different times had occasion to refer to two types of young people who are in their middle and upper teen years. One class is as pure and upright as Timothy, and the other class is as stubborn and rebellious as Rehoboam. Parents have the same duty to their teenage children that they have to their pre-teen children. They have authority over them and must exercise that authority in the way that will yield peaceable results. The teenaged child has the same responsibility to his parents that the younger child has to his. He is to honor and obey. Teenagers have not been given the assignment to bring up their parents, but the parents have been commanded to bring up their children. There must not be the shifting of the responsibility on the one hand or the usurping of it on the other. Teenagers should be loved, and they should be lovable. They can and should be the pride and joy of their parents. When they have been properly loved and disciplined from the cradle, there can be a pleasant hand-in-hand walk with their parents through these years of preparation for adulthood.

There is far too much being said in the church about the duty of "doing something for our young people," as though something special and different must be planned for this new species we have among us. The church is a teaching body, and it owes the same duty to every member, old and young. Teenagers are pupils and must be taught. It is the duty of elders, preachers, and teachers of classes to see that proper teaching is being done, and if it is then the church is fulfilling its duty to its young people.

The idea of obedience to parents carries over into many other walks of life. For instance, in the church there is the "over" and "under" relationship. (1 Thess. 5:12; Heb. 13:7,17.) The elders are "over" the flock and must guide properly. The members are "under" the elders and must obey. We never reach an age when we are not under the elders and when we are free to ignore their "rule" over us. We as Christians are children of God, and we are required to show our love, respect, and honor for Him by obeying every command that He has given to us.

In emphasizing the command "Children, obey your parents," we do well; but we must stop and consider the short phrase that follows. The command, as stated, says, "Children, obey your parents in the Lord." Without denying anything that we have said heretofore, we must say that the phrase "in the Lord" limits the submission. We must recognize that the word "all" in the command as stated earlier, "Children, obey your parents in all things," is a relative term and must be viewed in harmony with the expression "in the Lord." Whatever a child can do in the way of submission to his parents that in no way violates a law of God must be done. On the other hand, if the parent requires something of the child that is a clear violation of the will of God, then, as Peter and the other apostles once said concerning another matter, "We ought to obey God rather than men." (Acts 5:29.) When the child reaches the age of accountability before God, he becomes responsible for his own actions. Then even if it causes friction in the family, he must obey the Lord rather than his parents when there is a conflict in commands. Jesus said, "He that loveth father or mother more than me is not worthy of me ." (Matt. 10:37a.) God's will must come first. When one has had to sever his relationship with his family in order to serve the Lord, he will receive abundant blessings to recompense him for his loss. Jesus said, "There is no man that hath left house, or brethren, or sisters, or father, or mother, or wife, or children, or lands, for my sake, and the gospel's, but he shall receive an hundredfold now in this time, houses, and brethren, and sisters, and mothers, and children, and lands, with persecutions; and in the world to come eternal life." (Mk. 10:29,30.) A young man or a young woman may have to give up family ties in order to become a Christian, but Christ will make it turn out for good. Such a child is still honoring his parents, while at the moment he may be disobeying them. To honor means to give the proper esteem and credit due to them. If they, to the best of their ability, have trained him properly, he can still feel a debt of gratitude to them and show them respect and kindness. He owes them that in exchange for the care and love they have given even if there comes a time when they do not understand the stand he must take to be pleasing to the Lord. He honors them by standing for that which is right.

A child is to pay his own way in the family. That may sound like a peculiar statement to make when the child comes into the world naked and helpless. Yet, from the very beginning he is equipped to pay his own way. His ready smile and simple pleasures add an abundant joy to the life of his parents. As soon as he is able to express himself in the simplest words he can show his gratitude. Have you seen a very young child who had a new pair of shoes? He may hold one up to a perfect stranger with a smile and say the one word "shoe" and bring delight to all around. I

believe the most beautiful trait a child can develop is that
of gratitude, and it is a trait that should remain in one's
life until the very end. It adds pleasure to one's own life
and it brightens the world around. The lack of gratitude
brings unhappiness to all relatives, friends, and acquaint-
ances. I have a vivid memory of a child of perhaps ten or
eleven years of age with whom my wife and I were closely
associated when we were young. The mother tried hard to
please her only little daughter; perhaps she tried too hard.
She made neat, pretty little dresses for her and bought
matching shoes, and it seemed that everything was just as
it should be. We never heard the child say, "Thank you,"
or "I like it," or "It is pretty." She never liked anything
and complained and whined because there was something
else she wanted in the first place. She did not seem to
know how to show appreciation for anything. She was a
most unhappy child. It was truly pathetic.

A child costs the parents many, many dollars along the
way for clothes, food, doctors' bills, school expenses, and
many other such things, but he should not be made to feel
any debt for the expenses except the debt of gratitude. If
he has shown that gratitude by his big smiles and a hug
now and then, and if he has been obedient and trust-
worthy, he has paid his way, and the parents feel the wish
that they could do more instead of less for him.

My wife and I have two daughters. They have been and
still are the kind of daughters that make thinking of children's gratitude an easy and pleasant thing. I remember
when they were very small, my wife had made one of them
a little new dress. We had a visitor who came in, and the
child ran to him to show the new dress. She was so proud
of it that she had to share her joy. He observed her for a
bit and then said, "It must be a joy to make something for
a child like that." He was certainly right. The joy of having a new dress was not to be compared with the joy of
having made it for her since she was so grateful for it. She
more than paid the cost of the dress.

Do you see any likeness between the child in the home
who never expresses any word of thanks or shows any
gratitude for what is done for him and the child of God
who receives blessings upon numberless blessings without
ever showing any sign of thankfulness? God has blessed
us far above what we could ask or think. Do we appreciate
our blessings, or do we take them for granted? Do we

consider that they are our just due, that God owes them to us? I believe children in the home often think that their parents owe them the things they ask for. We hear sometimes that children do not ask to be born, and therefore the parents owe them whatever they desire. Parents do owe their children a great deal, but the children are not thereby free from the obligation of being grateful.

An earthly father delights in hearing his child say, "Thank you." Do you suppose our heavenly Father delights to hear the same? If we complain of everything that goes on in God's world and object to everything He does in nature, maybe we are not what He wants in His children. "Rejoice in the Lord always; and again I say, Rejoice. ... Be careful for nothing; but in everything by prayer and supplication with thanksgiving let your requests be made known unto God." (Phil. 4:4,6.)

When a grateful son or daughter comes to a mother with a request, she is eager to grant it. The price is paid by the thankfulness of the child. We never get too old to feel and show our debt of gratitude for all the parents have done for us. That love and gratitude ought to be expressed very freely, even when we no longer live in the house with our parents and when we ourselves are no longer young. It is nothing unusual for my wife and me to receive a letter from one of our daughters, who now has children of her own, in which she says, "I am glad that I am your daughter." Only a parent who has known the joy that such a message brings can understand what I mean. We have had occasion to give thanks to God many, many times for the love and gratitude that our daughters have shown. They have paid their way many times over, and they are our life insurance policies for our old age.

Children are our most precious possessions. Money, houses, lands, and other worldly things can in no way compare with them. They are a heritage of the Lord. They have souls that are worth more than the world itself. They are the parents' hopes for the future. They provide the security and protection for old age. They bring joy, happiness, and peace in this life which cannot be understood or duplicated in any other way. They are God's blessing to parents and should so regard themselves when they are old enough to think for themselves; and they should live in a way to show their obedience, love, respect, gratitude, and honor to their parents. In so doing they will be fitted

to meet whatever challenge life may present and be
pleasing to God now and in the after while.

"Even a child is known by his doings, whether his work
be pure, and whether it be right." (Prov. 20:11.)

Chapter 6

THE JOYS AND RESPONSIBILITIES
OF PARENTHOOD

Being a parent is one of the most important jobs in the world. It is a job for which few persons are really prepared. In giving the qualifications of an elder, his duties to his children are mentioned, and a question is asked which is significant. "If a man know not how to rule his own house, how shall he take care of the church of God?" (1 Tim. 3:5.) The implication is that it takes "know how" to be a good parent. There is "know how" involved in every job which a man undertakes, and the more knowledge he has of his job the better success he will make of it. If a man is working on complicated machinery, if he is farming, if he is a surgeon in the operating room, he needs to know something about the work he is doing. There are times when his life or the lives of others are involved, and there are great risks. Can you think of a more serious job than that of being a parent or any graver consequence of making a failure? When one fails in his secular job and suffers a loss of salary, it may bring financial hardships on his family, but the effects are only for this life. When one fails in his job as a parent he has jeopardized his own soul and the souls of his children. Being a parent is a serious matter, and it should be so considered by every young couple who enters into the marriage relationship. Children do not come into the home with a full set of pictured step-by-step directions for their training.

How can one prepare for this great undertaking? Where can he find instructions to guide him? The Bible is the best textbook that he can ever find on the subject. A

79

knowledge of the word of God and a respect for His law
will guide parents in their duties to their children just as in
every other walk of life. There are instructions in the Bible
concerning what to teach children and concerning admin-
istering proper discipline. There are many examples of
those who made successes of their job as parents and of
those who made failures. In the New Testament we have
the example of Eunice and Lois, the mother and grandmother in this case, who trained Timothy from his earliest
childhood into a knowledge of God. In the Old Testament
we have the example of Abraham of whom God said, "I
know him, that he will command his children and his
household after him, and they shall keep the way of the
Lord, to do justice and judgment." (Gen. 18:19a.) Then
there is the example of Eli who brought an end to his own
house because he made a failure in training his sons. God
said, "For I have told him that I will judge his house forever for the iniquity which he knoweth; because his sons
made themselves vile, and he restrained them not."
(1 Sam. 3:13.) In the previous chapter we are told of the
warning that God had given him. "Behold, the days come,
that I will cut off thine arm, and the arm of thy father's
house, that there shall not be an old man in thine house."
(1 Sam. 2:31.) These things are written for our learning.
They are to serve as our examples so that we can make a
success of this all important job of parenthood.

Things that are worthwhile in life are costly. We never
get anything of value for nothing. We expect to pay in
proportion to the value of that which we receive. The most
precious possession which a couple can have are their children. "Children are an heritage of the Lord: and the fruit
of the womb is his reward." (Ps. 127:1.) They are gifts
from the Lord and are of great value. They bring joy and
gladness to a home, but there are responsibilities that
come also. For these great gifts which become valuable
possessions, parents must pay a great price. We want to
notice some of the costs of parenthood.

One of the first costs that comes immediately to mind is
that of money. We usually think first of money when we
speak of what any object costs. Children cost money.
Every parent realizes that on the surface, but he may not
fully realize what it involves. "If any provide not for his
own, and specially for those of his own house, he hath
denied the faith, and is worse than an infidel." (1 Tim.

5:8.) There have been various estimates made on what it costs to bring a child from the cradle to adulthood. Every figure I have seen sounds so large that I immediately wonder how anybody could afford it; but it does not all have to be paid at one time, and little by little most parents find ways of doing it. There is food to buy, which must be planned for every day of every year. There are clothes to buy that have a way of wearing out too soon. School supplies must be bought again and again year after year. Necessities must be provided, and there must be a way found of forming a balance between necessary and extravagant spending. We need to learn somewhere along the way in life to be content with the simple things and not crave the extravagant luxuries for ourselves or for our children. If a parent cannot provide as much of the things that money can buy for his children as the neighbor down the street, he should not feel that he is depriving them if he provides more of those things that money cannot buy. He is not to feel that he must in some way, by going in debt or working an extra shift, get enough money to supply every desire of his children. That would be impossible, I suppose, no matter how much money is available. If a child thinks he can have whatever he desires simply by asking for it, there will be no end to his requests. The father must learn when to grant requests and when to deny them. He must learn to provide the necessities without complaining and without making the child feel guilty for making requests. On the other hand he must learn to deny the expensive non-essential things without feeling guilty himself for doing so.

One of the most precious things that parents owe their children is time. "And, ye fathers, provoke not your children to wrath: but bring them up in the nurture and admonition of the Lord." (Eph. 6:4.) Parents cannot "bring them up" unless they spend time with them, and a few minutes now and then will not suffice. It is a task that requires much time. There must be time just to talk. A child comes into the world with no knowledge of any kind. He has the potential for learning, but has everything to learn. His parents are his first and most important teachers. He starts to learn at birth, not at six years old when he starts to school. Dr. Burton L. White, head of Harvard University's internationally known preschool project, says that the first three years of a child's life are the most important in his entire period of development. He says that the developing and learning capacities that will see him through the rest of his life are pretty well set by the time he is three. I do not agree fully with his reasoning because I am sure it is possible to change one's direction later in life, but I do agree that the very early years are immensely important. It is then that the child learns the language and the feeling of security that can come only from constant association with his parents. He learns to respond to their expressions and moods, and he responds with his smiles and gurgles of pleasure or by his cries of distress.

In the 1960's there were many young people who formed mobs and created riots, that resulted in the burning of buildings on university campuses and along city streets. Violence and disorder were reported in every daily newspaper for a time. In so many cases, those young people were from homes where they had been neglected by their parents. They had never had laps to sit on or arms to cuddle them. They had not had the time and attention of their parents which they deserved. They had never been shown affection or had any one delight in their presence. They had had no one to be interested in their triumphs or to console them in their troubles. No one cared where they went or with whom they associated. No one told them they could not do what the crowd was doing. They grew up as though they had no parents, and they made their parents suffer for their neglect. They also inflicted suffering on innocent bystanders. Fathers cannot bring their children up unless they are with them a proper amount of time.

"Train up a child in the way he should go: and when he is old, he will not depart from it." (Prov. 22:6.) I have read articles on how trainers work with animals in the circus or for shows. Do you know what is the most important part of training? It is time. Just so, it takes time to properly train a child. An animal trainer must spend hours, days, months, and a few years training the animals to do a few simple tricks for the entertainment of a few people for a brief period of time. Parents must spend hours, days, months, and many years training their children, because they are working with souls that will live through an endless eternity. The task is momentous, but the joys and rewards are limitless.

In training children there are many things to be taught. Moses said to the children of Israel, "And these words, which I command you this day, shall be in thine heart: and thou shalt teach them diligently unto thy children, and shalt talk of them when thou sittest in thine house, and when thou walkest by the way, and when thou liest down, and when thou risest up." (Deut. 6:6,7.) We are not living under the law of Moses, but the things written there are preserved for our learning, and they happened by way of example. Our children should know the stories of the Old Testament. Then, since we do live under the New Testament law, they must know the things written there. Parents cannot teach children what they themselves do not know. It takes a great deal of study to be able to teach the Bible to the children, but it is one of the responsibilities of parenthood. There are parents who do not know the stories of Abraham, of Joseph, of David, of Ruth, and of Esther. They cannot teach them, and they are denying their children a great heritage. Moses said again, "The secret things belong unto the Lord our God: but those things which are revealed belong unto us and to our children for ever, that we may do all the words of this law." (Deut. 29:29.) The things that God revealed belong to us and they belong to our children. We must not hold back from them that which rightly belongs to them. We need the examples, the commandments, the promises, the warnings, and the whole counsel of God.

If we could ever come to have the proper concept of the importance of the word of God, we would find more time for study and for teaching what we learn to our children. These great lessons cannot be learned or taught some rainy Tuesday afternoon. Much time is involved. Some one may ask, How can any parent spend so much time with the children? What we are talking about requires much time. How is a busy mother or a tired father going to find the time to tell so many stories to the children? Before we answer the practical questions, let me say first that they had better find the time because God commanded it. If they were conscious enough of the seriousness of failing to teach, they might find time where they did not know it existed. A child demands attention. A busy mother must answer questions while she works. Did you know that a Bible story can be told while dishes are being washed or clothes ironed? The child can play with her doll

and listen as mother patiently washes the dishes. The
child will feel a part of the activity and can be very happy
to be in the room with her mother and have her attention.

If the television could be turned off some evening there
would be several hours of time to be with the children. The
children have been allowed to become slaves to the television set partly through the neglect of their parents. When
they are absorbed in the antics on the screen they are not
bothering parents with questions. At the same time they
are not learning anything of practical value. This matter
of spending time with children is of such major importance
that the parents could afford to sacrifice some of their
pleasures, some of the time they usually spend working,
or anything else necessary to devote attention to them.
The process of teaching which requires so much time must
begin early and continue throughout the entire period of
years that the child lives at home. This process of teaching
must include instruction in the word of God. Faith comes
of hearing and hearing of the word of God. The richest
inheritance that a parent can leave his child is a strong
faith in God. To fail to leave him this is to leave him poor
regardless of the material wealth that is left to him.

There is more involved in giving our children time than
just the teaching of the Bible. There must be time to talk
of many things, time to share his interests and to teach
him new interests. There should be time to build a strong
companionship together, a mutual feeling of respect. I do
not have a remarkable memory, but I can still recall little
incidents with my father when I was a child. The closeness
that we shared then has been pleasant to me to remember
all these many years later. A little boy misses a great deal
who does not have a chance to spend hours with his father
just talking together. I do not believe that all the benefit
is to the child, but I believe that the father is a better man
if he can learn to see the world through the eyes of a little
child. There is no generation gap between a worthy father
and an obedient son. If they are together often and share
the same pleasures and hardships, they are a great blessing to each other. The memories of the old man as he
comes near the end of the way can be very pleasant as he
remembers the joys shared with his son. Just so, the son,
as he reaches maturity, can enjoy thinking of the times he
spent with his father in talking and sharing, and he can
pass on the wisdom he learned to his own children. A

father needs to know his son, and the son needs to know his father. Each has a great deal to give to the other.

I have often thought as I have read the story of David's great grief over the death of his rebellious son Absalom that if the king had had time to spend with his son when he was growing up there might have been a different end to the story. David, as king, was naturally a very busy man with the burden of the kingdom on his shoulders, and he left his children to be raised without the strict hand of a father. The sweet singer of Israel wept bitterly when the news came from the battle, "The enemies of my lord the king, and all that rise against thee to do thee hurt, be as that young man is." If David had spent time in close friendship with his son he might have been spared his heartbroken cry, "O my son Absalom, my son, my son Absalom! Would God I had died for thee, O Absalom, my son, my son!" (2 Sam. 18.)

There are many lessons to be taught to children as they grow up around their parents' knees. They are to be taught obedience. First of all, they must learn to obey their parents. They will not learn the lesson by themselves. It must be taught carefully and consistently. The child must be brought into subjection. If a parent fails to do so, it is his own fault and not the fault of the child. An elder, in order to please God, must have his children in subjection with all gravity. (1 Tim. 3:4.) The child matures slowly so that there are twelve full months from one birthday to the next. What cannot be accomplished in one day may be done in days to follow. He will gradually learn to respect the parents' words if they are consistent and patient. Parents make many mistakes, but they must continue trying day after day until the child obeys promptly and pleasantly. I have suggested at times in illustrating the seriousness of failing to bring a child into subjection that a man could afford to take a year's leave of absence from his work, living on borrowed money, and spend his entire time at the task if it were necessary to accomplish the desired end. That is not necessary if both parents work toward the same goal and are in harmony in their discipline of the child.

In marriage two people become one. We may especially need to emphasize this oneness in the matter of discipline. It is sinful to abuse the child to the point of discouragement, frustration, and even hate. (Eph. 6:4; Col. 3:21.) It is also sinful to fail to make the proper use of the rod of chastisement. (Prov. 13:24; 19:18; Heb. 12:5-11.) Somewhere between the cruel abuse and the failure to chastise is the happy medium of chastening which yields the peaceable fruit of righteousness.

Mothers and fathers need to study the Bible on this matter and discuss it carefully before the children are born. This is a subject to pray about. There can be no success if one parent works against the other in the matter of discipline. There is "know how" involved. (1 Tim. 3:5.) Each one should know and believe what the Bible says, and each should give diligence to learn how to apply the principles.

Many families of children have been lost because of parental conflict on this subject which destroyed their chance to train them in the way they should go. If there are differences in judgment on some occasion, the parents should discuss the matter with patience, realizing the importance of unity of action. This discussion should be conducted in private when the children are not around. Parents must stand together or fail.

Please do not misunderstand the remarks that are now being made. Children should have careful supervision and strict discipline, but almost anything can be carried to an extreme. In the name of discipline some parents are cruel. They slap, beat, and scold until the children feel nothing but frustration and discouragement. Even the young have a keen sense of fairness, and they will not think more of parents who often punish them severely for slight wrongs. "Fathers, provoke not your children to anger, lest they be discouraged." (Col. 3:21.) "And, ye fathers, provoke not your children to wrath: but bring them up in the nurture and admonition of the Lord." (Eph. 6:4.)

Proper chastisement brings the peaceable fruit of righteousness. (Heb. 12:11.) Cruel and unreasonable punishment becomes abuse and will discourage children and drive them from home as soon as they are old enough to make it on their own. Beyond that, they may leave home to go out into society as bitter rebels against law, order, and the religion of Christ. The Christ was not to blame for their treatment, and neither was society in general, but the frustrated young people may turn against every symbol of law and authority. Have you seen this happen?

I have heard of a great preacher who has fought and is

fighting many battles for truth. His influence, as I know it, is very wholesome. I was astonished and saddened to learn that he has lost his children into the service of the devil. The one who told me explained the reason. He said, "No wonder, he was always abusive to his children when they came into his presence, and they were treated like dirt under his feet even when they were small."

If children are always crushed and embarrassed before visitors and always made to feel that they are in the way when they come into their father's presence when he is alone, they will be provoked and discouraged in the sense the inspired writers meant. Children are to be loved. They are not to be treated the way a cat treats a live mouse which it has caught and is not yet ready to eat.

Some parents are often pleasant with others outside the home and ready to accomodate neighbors in a very friendly way. At home they may be unkind and even abusive to their families. This is hard to explain. Are they mentally ill? There are some members of the church who appear kind and gentle in public who are unkind and insulting in the home. Why? Husbands are to love their wives and be not bitter against them. They are to honor them. Aged women are to teach the younger women to love their children. Why do some homes become places of terror, to which children dread returning after a day at school? Home should be a place to look forward to eagerly because there is some one there with whom they can share every experience of their day.

When a man destroys the peace and happiness of his own home, he has destroyed his own individual peace and happiness. He misses the love and joy that come to worthy parents. There must be a different feeling indeed in the heart of a father who returns home after a day on the job and have his children cower and hide from him and the one who is greeted with shouts of joy and gladness to see him. We ask again if men who abuse good wives and innocent little children are mentally sick or spiritually sick. They are definitely spiritually sick because they are violating the laws of God, but some of them, at least, may also be mentally sick.

Yes, indeed, parents are to provide careful supervision and firm discipline for their children, but neither should be carried to an extreme. The child that is just beginning to walk needs to be in his mother's sight almost every moment because he has not yet learned to avoid danger. As he grows a little older he can be trusted in the yard with traffic near, and gradually he learns the danger of the street and can be free to play for long periods of time using his imagination to provide entertainment for himself. His mother may check on him often, but she has loosened the apron strings.

There comes a time when well trained children may be free to go out with others their age. If they cannot be trusted in another home around the block with fine young people, they reflect a lack of proper training at home. Close supervision and firm discipline are not to keep them from having friends but to help them be able to make friends and to conduct themselves properly with them. Proper love and concern for children would certainly not require that they always stay at home so that they can be "supervised."

As the young are properly trained from birth through the various phases of growth, they can be trusted more and more, and they can be granted more and more freedoms to think for themselves and to make their own decisions. The loving, alert eyes of the parents are never closed to their behavior, and they owe to their children the realization that there is some one watching at all times, not to meddle, or criticize, or invade their privacy, but to advise, counsel, guide, and when necessary rebuke. The children must reach the point where they know the feelings of their parents so well that they can live good, clean, wholesome, and pure lives of their own choosing. The apron strings have become very slack now because they are no longer needed. If liberties of the right kind are not granted, the children will break the tie in a way to bring grief to themselves and their parents by going wild, having never learned self-discipline and how to use freedom.

Some fathers seem to feel that there are no other young people in the area who are good enough to associate with their children, and they forbid all such friends. Especially may this be true when children grow up to the time of pairing off boy with girl. The father may feel that no young man is good enough to date his daughter, so he keeps her at home to "supervise" her while the friends she has made at school away from home are having good times together. She feels left out, and she either rebels against her father and takes up with the first young man who notices her, or she may withdraw from her friends and yield to her father's demands so that she never marries. The father has shown a lack of wisdom, a lack of confidence in his own teaching, and a lack of trust in his daughter. His discipline has been extreme, unwise, and ridiculous. Little birds are to grow feathers, learn to fly, leave the nest, and build lives of their own. Children are to be given the proper home training that will prepare them for lives separate and independent of their parents.

From earliest childhood the child must be taught obedience to authority in every walk of life. He must be taught to obey his teachers in school. The teacher should demand the respect and obedience of the pupils. As a principal of schools for a number of years I have been amazed at which teacher could keep order in the classroom and which one could not. The children quickly sensed which one would allow disobedience and disturbance. The reflection is on both the teacher and the pupils when there is a constant disorder in a classroom. Parents have the responsibility of teaching the children that teachers are in authority and must be obeyed.

Children must be taught to obey the laws of the land. "Let every soul be subject unto the higher powers. For there is no power but of God: the powers that be are ordained of God. Whosoever therefore resisteth the power, resisteth the ordinance of God: and they that resist shall receive to themselves damnation." (Rom. 13:1,2.) This is a very important lesson to learn early in life. A father sets a very bad example before his son if he habitually breaks the speed laws and allows him to grow up thinking that it is the smart thing to do to outwit the highway patrol officer. Since civil government is ordained of God, it follows that any resistance to it is resistance against God. The rulers are appointed for the protection of the good and for the punishment of the evil.

Children should be taught that there is a penalty to pay for every act of disobedience, whether it is disobedience to God, to parents, or to any other authority. The fear of punishment is one reason then for obedience. The second reason for obedience is love for the one in authority. The child comes to love his parents because of his dependence on them and because they represent security and protection. The laws of the land are also for one's security and protection. The child should be so grounded in the spirit of obedience that his conscience will keep him from disobedience. Just as there are penalties to pay if the child disobeys his parents, his teachers, or the officers of the law, just so there are penalties for disobeying the spiritual laws of God. The child must early be taught that, and parents cannot teach if they have not learned the lesson themselves. A disobedient child is a disappointment to all who see him. It is sometimes hard to carry on a conversation in a room with adults when such a child is also in the room, because he whines, cries, or shows some act of rebellion that disrupts the thoughts of all.

One of the most important things of all that the parent owes his children is love. Love is a deep feeling of sincere interest in the welfare of the children. Children need love, and they must have it in order to become the kind of adults they should be. They are secure and happy if they are loved. The proper love on the part of the parent will cause him to guide and train his child properly. The lack of love leads to a lack of discipline which leads to an insecure and unhappy child. I have known parents who said they loved their child too much to punish him. That is not a sign of love. It is a sign of weakness and neglect. The child's entire character lies in his parents' hands. It is in their power to mold him into any form they choose. I read a book a long time ago which pictured a young couple as they stood beside the bassinet in which lay their tiny son. They said to one another, "Let us make man." Of course, the expression is used in another sense when God said in the beginning, "Let us make man in our image," but the book was picturing the challenge that faced the young parents as they recognized their responsibility in building the character of that infant into a worthy man. It is indeed a grave responsibility, but it can be met.

"He that spareth his rod hateth his son: but he that loveth him chasteneth him betimes." (Prov. 13:24.) I knew a family once who had lost a little boy and had been very grieved, as other parents would be, over his death. As the young mother thought back over the years she had had him she remembered having punished him for his childish misdemeanors. She decided, in her grief, that she had done wrong to punish him. She promised the Lord if He would give her another child she would never punish him. The Lord gave her other children, but I do not believe

He did so because of her foolish promise. I must say however that she kept her promise. At the time I was associated with her she had a preschool child that neither she, nor the father, nor the baby sitter could control. She could not take him to the services of the church because he disturbed so badly that nobody in the building could worship. When the baby sitter took him into the yard to play, she had to keep him in a leather harness to prevent his running into the street. He was then four years old, but she could not tell him what to do. He would not obey. She had to guide him by a harness. He had never been punished. The poor foolish mother thought she loved him too much to punish him, but Solomon said she was showing hate instead of love. The father in that family found things to do after work to keep him away from home, and I could hardly blame him. I would not have wanted to spend an evening in the room with the child. Yes, I do blame the father. He was the head of that home, and he should have acted like it. He should have taken the initiative in seeing that the child was properly disciplined. If there had been time given to him and interest shown from his birth, there would not have been such a situation that seemed almost hopeless before he was even old enough to go to school. The child was too young to make his own decisions and to be responsible for his own actions, so the burden of his behavior rested on the parents. He was an innocent child and was to be pitied. Parents owe proper discipline to their children. Do you think that child was constantly laughing? He was just the opposite, always frowning, crying, and pouting. He was an insecure child who had no guidelines. He needed restraint and boundary lines set for him so he could feel protected and loved. "Chasten thy son while there is hope, and let not thy soul spare for his crying." (Prov. 19:18.) This implies that there may come a time when hope of reaching him will be gone. The chastisement that every normal child needs would have made him a joy to himself, his parents, and to all the neighbors. A son that is not disciplined is like a child that has no father. He is greatly to be pitied. (Heb. 12:8.)

The child is like a mound of potter's clay. The potter can take the clay and fashion it into whatever form he chooses. He can then dry and temper it, and the form is set into its permanent shape. That is a frightening thought. As the

twig is bent, so the tree is inclined. As the child is molded
and shaped, so will the man be. The challenge is very
great when the parents realize that they have the power to
shape the very eternal destiny of the soul that inhabits the
body of their little child. How many parents will be lost
because they failed in their duty to their children? Parents
will be judged for the way they have directed their
children as well as for every other deed they have done.

Most parents wish their children to be successful in life,
but the definition of success may vary exceedingly. Some
think of success as being wealthy. When I was in high
school and even in college, we had to assemble each day in
the auditorium for a devotional period, and we had talks
from various business men, preachers, and politicians in
the area. Most of them tried to inspire the students to
make a success in life. As I look back on those talks, it
seems to me that we were fed a steady diet of a poor boy
who became rich. That was success. Is that what you, as
parents, think of as success when you look in the bassinet
at your infant? If he is able to amass a fortune and gain
worldly recognition, will he necessarily be a successful
man? What is success? Jesus said it is hard for a rich man
to enter the kingdom of heaven. Surely no right thinking
father would wish his son to jeopardize his soul in order to
gain riches. On the other hand, that may be the very
example that the father is daily setting before his son. The
dollar mark may be the idol that is set up in the home to be
worshipped.

What is success? I remember reading that after Moses'
death, the Lord spoke to Joshua, who had been chosen to
take Moses' place as leader of the children of Israel, and
He said to him, "This book of the law shall not depart out
of thy mouth; but thou shalt meditate therein day and
night, that thou mayest observe to do according to all that
is written therein: for then thou shalt make thy way prosperous, and then thou shalt have good success." (Josh.
1:8.) To know and to do the will of the Lord would be
counted success in the eyes of the Lord. I have often wondered how many parents among the people of God have
looked into the face of their little child and hoped that he
might one day preach the gospel. I have been preaching
for forty five years, and I can truthfully say that I have
never wished that I had done some other work in life. It
may not be as lucrative a work as many others would be,

but it pays far more in fringe benefits than any other I can think of. I think of the fringe benefits as being the association with and the friendship of the finest people on earth. There are parents who would be ashamed and embarrassed if their son should tell them that he had decided to preach the gospel. Why? Because their interests are in worldly things, and neither they nor their friends are concerned with spiritual things. They had rather their son and their daughter do those things that are acceptable to the crowd. They do not want them to be unpopular. They may allow them to do things in school or at the game or at the party which they know are sinful or at least questionable rather than risk the loss of popularity. Goodness has never been popular with the world. It may walk a rather lonely path at times, but it leads in the right direction.

I am reminded of a passage of scripture from the sermon on the mount: "Enter ye in at the strait gate: for wide is the gate, and broad is the way, that leadeth to destruction, and many there be that go in thereat: because strait is the gate, and narrow is the way, which leadeth unto life, and few there be that find it." (Matt. 7:13,14.)

The popular way may be very pleasant and there may be many companions for a time, but it does not lead in the right direction. The narrow way may not be as pleasant from a worldly point of view, and definitely there will not be as many travelers, but it has a bright place at the end. Those who are in that narrow road are the successes in life because they have the promise of another life. There are far too many parents who are willing to push their children out into things that are dangerous and yet they are the things that lead to popularity. They are pushing them into the crowd that is in the broad way that leads to destruction. They should be shielding them from the dangers and pitfalls of that broad way and teaching them to choose friends because of their character and not because they are accepted by the crowd. They should be taught to look for quality and not quantity. Let them be a little lonely at times rather than compromise character.

A mother and a father can do more with that little bundle of clay that has been given to them by the Lord than they may realize. They can mold it into something that can give them joy, happiness, and honest pride if they will take enough time and effort. They need to realize that they cannot do what should be done for the child without the help of the One who gave him to them. They must spend much time in the study of God's word and in prayer for His guidance in their major undertaking. They will make mistakes even when trying hard to do right. Other parents make mistakes also. Then they all have to try again.

Children must be taught to work, and they must be taught the dignity of work. Very early in life a child must be taught that he is part of a family unit and that he must bear his share of the responsibility for making it the right kind of home. As soon as a child is able to toddle to his toy box and get his toys for himself, he is old enough to help put them away. He needs to know that the toys belong at a certain place when they are not being used. He will not learn the lesson in one day, but all knowledge comes a little at a time. As he grows a little older he can learn to help his mother make his bed, pick up his clothes, and tidy up his room. I will admit that his first efforts are very feeble, but he is with his mother. She is talking with him all the time, and he is learning from her. He likes to be part of all that is going on around him, and it is surprising how early his efforts become more skilled.

In being taught to work, a child learns that nothing of value comes without effort. He learns that the world does not owe him anything, but that he owes something to the world. The lessons he learns as a child will be remembered in adulthood. If he is taught to shun work, to regard it as degrading and undignified, he will not be a good provider when he is the head of a family of his own. He must be taught that the only honorable way to obtain money for himself is to work for it. The apostle Paul wrote the brethren at Thessalonica and told them, "For even when we were with you, this we commanded you, that if any would not work, neither should he eat." (2 Thess. 3:10.)

There is no substitute for parents. There is no way a child can be brought up to be a normal, well adjusted person without parents. I remember many years ago going into a house where there were several thousand baby chickens. They had never seen a mother hen. Now, I have discovered that baby chickens do very well that way. They do not need to hear the cluck of a mother hen. Brought up that way, being fed food that is carefully balanced for nutrition by scientific experts, they grow quickly and are ready for market in a surprisingly short time. There is a vast difference in raising chickens and in raising children. If you put a hundred fifty children in a brooder type home and feed them properly balanced food and clothe them with the best of clothes, they may still grow up to be neurotic. They miss the lap to sit on. They miss the arms to hold and cuddle them. They miss the individual attention which children need to feel secure and happy. If you will talk with some one from an area where there is an institutional orphan home, he will likely tell you that it is almost impossible to teach a Bible class when there are children in it from the orphan home. They are so starved for attention that they demand it in class and have to be in the limelight. They have been taught certain Bible facts that they can say from memory, and they want to show off their knowledge.

The Lord put children in families, and when a home unit is destroyed by death or desertion, there are other homes that can and are eager to care for the children. When Lot's father Haran died, Lot lived with his uncle Abraham. When Esther's parents died, she lived with her cousin Mordecai. There need to be parents who have the time and love to give to each child as an individual and make him feel that he is important. Chickens can be brought up very satisfactorily in brooder type homes, but children are of more value than chickens. They have souls that are worth more than the world itself, and they must have proper care and training to develop into the kind of adults that will be acceptable to God.

There are many responsibilities to face as parents, but there are joys and rewards that make it a wonderful experience to be a father or a mother. My wife and I have many, many happy memories of our two little girls as they were learning to talk, taking their first faltering steps, starting to school, running to meet a weary father at the end of the day, growing into girlhood, on into mature women, and now raising their own little families. They have paid their way by their gratitude and love. They are our social security for our old age. They will not fail in their duty to us then because they have not failed in other things that have been required of them through the years.

Parents should enjoy their children. They should rejoice in their triumphs and console them in their troubles. There should be a mutual sharing of interests and a closeness that bridges any generation gap of which society around may talk. The home can be a wonderful place if parents and children enjoy being together and love one another properly.

The rewards are many, and they last for a long time. In fact, the most precious memories that an elderly man or woman can have are those of the time when their children were little and constantly around their feet. That was the time when the parents were needed so much, and there is always something pleasant about being needed. If the home life is what it should be, the rewards and joys outweigh the troubles and sorrows along the way.

It is fitting that we use here a verse from the Psalms that we have thought of in connection with the child's place in the home. "Lo, children are an heritage of the Lord: and the fruit of the womb are his reward. As arrows are in the hand of a mighty man; so are children of the youth. Happy is the man that hath his quiver full of them: they shall not be ashamed, but they shall speak with the enemies in the gate." (Ps. 127:3-5.)

Chapter 7

WHY ARE THERE SO MANY DIVORCES?

It is alarming, not just to religious people, but also to civic minded people, that the American home is about to be destroyed. The home is a very essential, basic unit of our society, and if the home is destroyed then the nation will be destroyed. It is an institution that was planned by God in the very beginning of time. God created Adam and placed him in the Garden of Eden and made Eve to be his help meet, thus forming the first home ever known on the earth. The home is not parallel to the church because Christ purchased the church with His own blood. It is His body, and the salvation of our souls is found in the body of Christ. So far, however, as this world and human relationships are concerned, there is no more important unit of society than the home.

The nation depends on the products of the home, the children that are born and reared there. Yet, today there are thousands of homes that are being disrupted and destroyed by divorce. In some cities in certain years there are more divorces granted than there are marriage licenses. In the nation as a whole a large percentage of the marriages end in divorce, and of those that do not a large percentage are not happy and are kept together for reasons other than love and respect of the partners for one another. That the situation now is worse than a few decades ago is beyond all doubt. The facts are too well known for question. Why has the situation changed? Some may answer that there are more people now. That is true, but we are talking about percentages. There are more divorces in proportion to the number of marriages than ever before in our country. That is the alarming truth that we are now concerned about.

Why are there so many divorces? I believe I can answer the question in one sentence. There has been a breakdown in faith. Now, we will enlarge on that and explain why we believe that to be the basic cause for the destruction that has come in the home unit, but everything we say will come back in the end to the one reason: There has been a breakdown in faith. Too many people no longer believe in God, so they no longer believe that the Bible is His word. If it is not His word, it has no spiritual value to us today. It is the product of men with no divine authority. Some may say that it contains good moral principles, and it tells of the lives of good men, but it is not really the word of God but is only the word of a group of men. Other books would then be of as much value to us if such were true.

Some one has well said that if one does not believe the first four words of the Old Testament, he does not believe any of the sixty six books of the Bible. The first four words are: "In the beginning God." Of course, that is not a complete sentence, but if one does not believe that in the beginning there was God, he certainly cannot believe the remainder of the sentence. "In the beginning God created the heavens and the earth." (Gen. 1:1.) Our children are taught on television, even on those programs especially adapted to them and arranged in cartoons to catch the fancy of the very, very young, that everything is here by chance. Evolution is taught so that when they reach school age they are ready to accept the theories taught by their textbooks and encyclopedias. Some teachers quite boldly deny the Bible account of creation. The hand of God is left out, and everything began by chance and has continued by evolution. If the Bible is not an authoritative work then we are without a compass to guide us in our behavior. That is what has happened to our country.

"O ye of little faith," our Savior often said to his little inner circle of disciples. We are reminded of a strict warning given by the writer of the book of Hebrews, "Take heed, brethren, lest there be in any of you an evil heart of unbelief, in departing from the living God." (Heb. 3:12.) It is possible even for a child of God who has been strong in the faith to allow an "evil heart of unbelief" to arise in him so that he departs from God. The farther he goes from God the less respect he will have for what God says.

In the very first two verses of the book of Hebrews we are told: "God, who at sundry times and in divers manners spake in time past unto the fathers by the prophets, hath in these last days spoken unto us by his Son." God hath spoken. Do you believe that there is a God and that He has spoken to us? If so, do you believe that what He has said is important? He has spoken on many subjects, and He has spoken on the subject of divorce. We would do well to consider carefully what he has said on the subject if we believe that what He has said is important.

In a former chapter we have given emphasis to God's law of marriage. It is stated simply, "Whosoever shall put away his wife, saving for the cause of fornication, causeth her to commit adultery: and whosoever shall marry her that is divorced committeth adultery." (Matt. 5:32.) Now, the Bible deals with the sin of divorce. Adultery and fornication are listed in a few different catalogues of sins, such as in 1 Cor. 6:9,10; Gal. 5:19-21; Col. 3:5. They are classed as sins that will keep one out of heaven. Heaven is denied to those who are guilty, and yet they are the very sins that are involved in divorce. There cannot be a divorce and remarriage without at least one party's being guilty of the sin of adultery or fornication. If the divorce were not a direct result of fornication or adultery, there would yet be the sin if one partner remarries.

So often when a very young couple marries, a very trivial thing arises over which they disagree. Not having been grounded in the seriousness of the marriage bond, they divorce. Soon they both remarry in violation of God's law. The older they get, the more they may think of the condition in which they are living. If either of them comes to have faith in God and in His word, there must of necessity arise doubts and questions about the marriage. Life would become unbearable in that situation. I may not know how to say it, and I may not even know what ought to be said, but I wish people could believe that what the Bible has to say about marriage and divorce is very serious and that it should be taken at face value. There is coming a judgment day when all will stand before God and be judged according to the deeds done in the body. "For we must all appear before the judgment seat of Christ; that every one may receive the things done in his body, according to that he hath done, whether it be good or bad." (2 Cor. 5:10.) If the fornicator and adulterer cannot be heirs of heaven, then the subject of divorce is a very serious one to consider.

There are so many divorces because people have laid the Bible on the shelf as if it were of no value. They have ignored it and they have nothing left to guide their lives except animal instinct. If there were some way, as if by magic, to fill every heart with great faith, as Peter would say, "precious faith" (2 Pet. 1:1), there would be an immediate drop in the number of divorces. More faith, fewer divorces. That is a very simple solution to the problem. The thing to do to solve the problem then is for every parent to instill in every child the kind of "unfeigned faith" that Eunice and Lois instilled in Timothy. That is the genuine kind. You would not expect a man like Timothy to divorce his wife. Such a young man would choose to begin with a mate of similar character who would have the same strong faith. Then the two of them would have the respect for God's word which would cause them to make a success of their marriage. People of that type are not the ones who get the divorces.

From a child Timothy had known the holy scriptures. (2 Tim. 3:15.) If parents will take their children and fill their hearts with the word of God and build a respect for the very fact that God has spoken, they will be guarding them against the sin of divorce. Teaching them the word of God will include teaching them His law of marriage and the sanctity of the marriage vows. There has not been enough teaching on the subject by aged women as they teach younger women, by teachers in classes, by preachers in the pulpits, and by mothers and fathers around the fireside in their own homes. Faith comes by hearing, and hearing by the word of God. If a child ever comes to have faith it will be because he has heard the word of God. There has been a lack of teaching, so there has been a lack of faith arise. The breakdown in faith has led to the divorce evil of our day.

The preachers over the land have to bear a great load of guilt in allowing the breakdown in faith. No other class of people is exempt, but preachers have the responsibility of standing before audiences often to speak. What they speak will determine to a great extent what the audience believes. Too many young preachers in various religious groups of our day go off to a Seminary somewhere to learn how to preach. Likely while there they will sit at the feet of infidels and atheists. Their teachers may scoff at the record of the creation. They may ridicule the story of Abraham and Sarah and their child of promise. They may laugh at the idea of the Israelites' crossing the Red Sea on dry land. Almost certainly they will deny the virgin birth and the resurrection of our Lord. They make man only an animal with no God and no Heaven. The young preachers come back home with little or no faith and stand before audiences to entertain or to moralize on some popular civic subject.

A few years ago I was in another state conducting a gospel meeting and was staying with the local preacher. One day he left me sitting in his car in town while he ran into a place of business expecting to be gone only a few minutes. His minutes stretched out into quite a long period of time. When he returned he told me why he was delayed. One of the employees in the business wanted to talk with him because he was greatly distressed. He had just received a letter from the son who had grown up at his house to be a fine, conscientious man with plans to preach for the denomination in which he had been reared. The father had sacrificed to send him to a seminary where he could learn to preach. Now had come a letter saying that he no longer believed the Bible to be the inspired word of God. He did not believe that Jesus was born of a virgin, although the Bible clearly states that He was. He thought that the Bible was written by men who were feeling after truth and searching for it. He thought that in this enlightened age we have learned things that they did not know. The Bible had been taken from him. What could he preach when he stood in the pulpit before an audience that was ready to believe whatever he said? No, he had not given up his intention to preach. He had just changed his mind on what there was to preach. What could he say if he left the Bible out of his sermons? How sad!

When religious people lose their faith and stop leaning on a "Thus saith the Lord," there will be a breakdown in moral principles. When religious people stop believing that "God hath spoken," then every man becomes a law unto himself, and there is nothing right or wrong except as each man's conscience may determine. A man's conscience is a product of his teaching, and if he has had no teaching of the Bible principles of right or wrong he is left without much conscience to guide him. Naturally, if there is no God, or if there is a God who set the earth in motion and left it, then certainly He has not said anything of importance for us today about marriage or anything else. A breakdown in faith is the big problem facing us right now. It is not a new problem.

"Wherefore seeing we also are compassed about with so great a cloud of witnesses, let us lay aside every weight, and the sin that doth so easily beset us, and let us run with patience the race that is set before us, looking unto Jesus, the author and finisher of our faith." (Heb. 12:1,2a.) "The sin that doth so easily beset us" is the sin of unbelief. Now if we can believe that Jesus is the Christ, the Son of God, and that God has spoken unto us through His Son, if we are taught what the Son has said until we have laid up His word in our hearts so that we might not sin against Him, and if our hearts are filled with a respect for the authority of Christ, then that is the surest guarantee I know against divorce. An awareness that all things are naked and laid open before the eyes of Him with whom we have to do would make people take thought to their moral behavior. If we commit sins that will lead to divorce, God knows about them.

Modernism, as we call it, which is plain old infidelity, was rampant in America at the time of the American Revolution. Tom Paine thought that the Bible would be laid on the shelf and it was the Age of Reason. Benjamin Franklin thought there was a God who created the earth but that He does not hear us pray and the Bible is not His word. He thought that He set the world in motion and left it just as a manufacturer has no knowledge of the car after it is sold. In Yale University about that time, which was then a school for preachers, there were two young men of all the student body who believed that Christ was born of a virgin. After the turn of the century into the 1800's there came a great awakening and a revival of interest in the Bible. I like to think that a similar situation will arise again. If there is some way to wake people up and get the faith back, there will be an improvement in the divorce situation. Homes would stay together if there were more respect for what God says.

A breakdown in faith manifests itself in various ways. There are situations in modern life that invite dangers to the marriage relationship. There is a powerful sentence in the New Testament that has only two words in it. It says,

"Flee fornication." (1 Cor. 6:18.) Run from it. The sin that has the greatest power to destroy a home is the sin of fornication. There are several words which fit into the same class to describe this sin. There are "uncleanness" and "filthiness" used in Ephesians 5:3,4. "Uncleanness" and "lasciviousness" are used together in the same verse with "adultery" and "fornication" in Galatians 5:19. In Romans 1:31, the term "without natural affection" is used. The descriptions in which these words are used are not of the attraction of one man for one woman, but they are used of such characters that Peter would call "natural brute beasts." (2 Peter 2:12.) Such are like animals. They satisfy their passions with no regard for right or wrong. In schools the boys and girls are taught that we all evolved from some little one cell something that came to life by chance and when we die that is the end. There is no here-after, therefore while we are in this life we should do what-ever satisfies our lusts and appeals to our passions. That is the end to which a breakdown in faith leads.

Fornication is one of the most common sins of our day. In the *Reader's Digest* in an article entitled, "Ten Questions Couples Ask Marriage Counselors Most," (June 1976) there is this statement: "Statistics show that one out of two husbands and one out of five wives have been unfaithful at least once." I do not know how the statistics were obtained, and I do not know if they are accurate; but even if they are grossly exaggerated, there remains an alarming situation in our society. In this same article a marriage therapist Nathan Hurvitz is quoted as saying, "In many instances unfaithfulness is a message about something wrong in the marriage." We ordinarily use the word "adultery" when we speak of unfaithfulness in marriage and the word "fornication" to refer to immoral conduct between unmarried couples. The Bible makes no distinction between the words. Jesus said, "Whosoever shall put away his wife, saving for the cause of fornication, causeth her to commit adultery: and whosoever shall marry her that is divorced committeth adultery." (Matt. 5:32.)

Today fornication, whether between married or un-married couples, is not only tolerated but is often recommended in high circles. I have already had occasion to refer to a statement that was made on public television by the First Lady of our country in which she stated her approval of her unmarried daughter's having an illicit love affair. She had the lack of judgment to say she believed there would be fewer divorces if there were more such affairs. Professors in some universities advocate trial marriages—try this one, and if it does not work, try some one else. To send a son or daughter to some of the heavily endowed universities of our day is very much like pitching him or her into a den of lions. We are speaking from a moral and spiritual point of view. The Bible does not recommend fornication! Can you see the connection between a breakdown in faith and a breakdown in morals? A couple may take vows before God to live together in marriage. Then one becomes unfaithful to the other. The home is destroyed and at least one soul, likely two, three, or even four souls are lost in eternity. Such is the seriousness of the sin of infidelity—fornication, if you please. We need to give a great deal of thought to the subject and spend much time talking about the danger to our children.

Our modern industrial situation has led women out of the home. A number of things would encourage car pooling, so a carload of people, some men, some women, ride to and from work every day together. They get to the place of business, and they work together all day—a man at this machine, a woman at that machine beside him. The talking together may become suggestive, and soon temptation arises. One or both may be too weak to resist, and two souls may be lost. If the husband and wife lived together and worked together as the farmer and his wife did in pioneer America, there would be fewer temptations and hence fewer divorces.

Most of us have seen this unnatural situation in the work of the doctor and his nurse. A doctor needs a nurse, one who can be at his beck and call for eight or more hours and be always courteous to him and to his patients. He would not want her if she were not courteous, so she puts on a pleasant face regardless of her feelings. She is right by his elbow as he operates, ready to hand him the instrument he needs before he can ask for it. She is skilled, efficient, and always pleasant. He works beside her for long hours until he is worn to the bone with fatigue, and still she is courteous. He goes home to a wife who has borne the strain of caring for the house and children, and who is not being paid a good salary for her smiles, so he finds her tired and disappointed that he did not get there in time to receive the guests whom he may have invited for dinner. She is tired, and he is tired, and their nerves are frayed to the breaking point. She nags and criticizes. Soon he divorces his wife and marries his nurse because he imagines that she never grows impatient or unpleasant. He did not see her when she reached home after a hard day at work, as she went by the babysitter's house, picked up her child, stopped by the supermarket to get the quickest thing to be bought for dinner, went home where she had to cope with a child who was starved for a mother's attention and a husband who had a fuss with his boss and was threatening to change jobs. There is a meal to prepare, clothes to launder, and the house to clean. She thinks how nice it would be to be married to some one who could afford to hire a maid for her and who would never frown or scold. So, two homes are destroyed. That situation, with other details, has been played on the stage of life hundreds upon hundreds of times.

The business man marries his secretary; the man at the plant marries the woman who works at the next machine. A doctor needs a nurse; a business man needs a secretary; the man and woman have a right to work in the plant; but there is grave danger when this woman's husband works side by side all day long with that man's wife. If working conditions are pleasant, as every business seeks to make them, then there may be temptations arise that only the strongest can resist. We are all human, and the man who vowed to be faithful to his wife until death and planned beyond all doubt to keep his vow may find the temptation too strong. The woman who married the man she loved and planned sincerely to remain faithful to the end of life may be swept off her feet by a smooth-tongued flatterer on the job.

I heard this story a long time ago, and although I am sure most of you have heard some version of it, it illustrates the point I am trying to make. A man was working at a sawmill, and his work kept him close beside a big circular saw. The saw was spinning with enormous power and speed. The slightest awkward movement could cost an arm or perhaps a life. Some one said to him, "Aren't you afraid to work here by that saw?" He replied, "I certainly am. If I were not, it would be dangerous."

I would like to point out to everybody who works in any dangerous moral condition that he should be afraid for his very soul. He should realize that he can be destroyed if he makes a misstep. He will not be as likely to stumble and fall into a pit from which he cannot escape if he is very much aware that it exists. If a young lady has been taught discretion and chastity, if she knows there is a God to whom she must give an account of her conduct, and if she has great strength of character, then perhaps she can work there as a nurse side by side with the doctor or across the desk from her boss; but both of them need to be conscious of the danger and do a lot of praying. They must both be sure that there is never any indiscreet talk or action that could arouse lascivious thoughts. Lasciviousness leads to the overt act of fornication, so they should be afraid of it just as the man should be afraid of that powerful circular saw.

"Know ye not that the unrighteous shall not inherit the kingdom of God? Be not deceived: neither fornicators, nor idolaters, nor adulterers, nor effeminate, nor abusers of themselves with mankind, nor thieves, nor covetous, nor drunkards, nor revilers, nor extortioners, shall inherit the kingdom of God." (1 Cor. 6:9,10.) He says, "Be not deceived." He can be led so unwarily into danger that it behooves all of us to be on guard and walk with our eyes open, seeing every step of the way. After naming all those grievous sins of the flesh, the writer spent verse after verse on the sin of fornication. Now, he does not say that fornication is the most serious sin of them all, because any one will make one lose heaven, but he did single it out for special attention, and he said, "Flee fornication. Every sin that a man doeth is without the body; but he that committeth fornication sinneth against his own body." (v. 18.) Do not invite it by unholy talk or actions.

Why are there so many divorces in America today? In the seventh chapter of Proverbs a young man is described who is void of understanding. He went and knocked at the door of a woman who came to meet him dressed in the attire of a harlot. It does not describe her clothing, but she was dressed so that when Solomon looked out his window and saw her he knew by her attire that she was a harlot. In the book of Genesis there is a story in the life of Judah in which he went in unto his own daughter-in-law without recognizing her. She was dressed in the attire of a harlot. She had "covered herself with a veil and wrapped herself." She was dressed so as to completely hide her identity. He

thought her to be a common prostitute. The veil she wore
to conceal her identity indicated that she was a harlot.
(Gen. 38.) Now, styles change from one age to another,
but a woman can always advertise her character by her
attire. There may be women, and I am confident that
there are, who are not immoral who yet dress in such a
way as to arouse lust in the hearts of those of the opposite
sex who see them walking down the street. The scantily
clothed body is an invitation to lust. The great man David
saw Bathsheba taking a bath, and he lusted after her. The
sin of lust led to adultery, which led to murder. The king
of Israel fell, and great was the effect of his fall. If Bathsheba had closed her drapes and taken her bath in private,
that story would never have taken place. I am not excus-
ing David. God did not excuse him, and he did not excuse
himself. He was man enough when his sin had been driven
home to him to say, "I have sinned," but let us not overlook Bathsheba's part in the story. She had to suffer for
the sin just as he did. God smote their child so that he
died. The effect of the sin was far-reaching. The prophet
said that David had given occasion to the enemies of the
Lord to blaspheme. (2 Sam. 11,12.)

I often have occasion to speak on the clothing of women,
and I usually read 1 Timothy 2:9,10, "In like manner also,
that women adorn themselves in modest apparel, with
shamefacedness and sobriety; not with broided hair, or
gold, or pearls, or costly array; but (which becometh
women professing godliness) with good works." As I have
pointed out in another chapter, there are some who would
insist that the word "modest" does not mean what we
ordinarily have in mind when we use it, but rather that it
means "appropriate." Well, very good. I would certainly
not think it appropriate for a woman to appear in public
almost completely unclothed. We have already shown in
another place that we can well dismiss the word "modest"
for our purpose in speaking of clothing, because we still
have the word "shamefacedness" or "shamefastness."
That will take care of any objection. There should be "a
sense of shame, modesty" in the demeanor of women professing godliness. There should be "that modesty that is
'fast' or rooted in the character." (W. E. Vines, *An Expository Dictionary of New Testament Words.*)

I have talked with women about their clothing, and I
have had some say, "Why do you not talk more to the

men?" I answer by saying, "Because I find more in the Bible about women." Evidently, judging from the way the Bible deals with the matter, the man's exposed body would not tempt a woman to lust to the same degree that a woman's exposed body would tempt a man. She will get attention if she walks down the street dressed like a harlot. I believe any woman with a small measure of common sense can know when she is dressed like a harlot. If she is not a harlot she should not dress like one. That is false advertising. A truck driver pulled his truck to a stop one day on the street by a sidewalk where a woman was walking "in the attire of a harlot." He called to her in language that was very unbecoming on his part and insulting to her. She was highly offended. He said, "If you are not that kind, why are you advertising?"

If we could get American women to put their clothes back on, there would be fewer divorces. I will say, in passing, that men should keep their clothes on also. There is such a thing as decency, and it ought to be respected. There is so much nudity on the streets and on television that it is a disgrace to our society. Shows are coming into the home that have displays of scantily clothed bodies that are intended to entertain by creating lust. Lust leads to fornication. If there were less lust there would be less fornication. If there were less fornication there would be fewer divorces. More respect for God's word would take care of the whole lascivious problem. The stylist who introduced the mini-skirt admitted that it was designed to have sex appeal. In America the number of reported rapes increased drastically the year the mini-skirt was introduced. If there has ever been anything more disgraceful or more like the attire of a harlot, I am glad I was not around to see it. Every man has within him a God-given instinct that is holy and right in its proper use. The same is true of the woman. The instinct that causes a man to be attracted to a woman and a woman to a man helps to make the marriage tie strong and helps to keep them together. The suggestion is made in 1 Corinthians 7:2, "To avoid fornication, let every man have his own wife, and let every woman have her own husband."

Why are there so many divorces? Because there is so much indecency of attire. Modesty has just been forgotten, and chastity is becoming an obsolete word. Mothers are not teaching their daughters to be chaste and discreet.

Mothers are the ones who buy the clothing for their daughters, so whatever the daughter wears is a reflection of good or evil on the mother. Be careful, mother, that you do not lead your daughter into the very sins that you should be teaching her to avoid.

Alcohol and other drugs have become a major problem in our nation. Alcohol is the most dangerous of the drugs because it is the most common, and it has become acceptable in the highest levels of society. It is advertised on radio and television. It is advertised in full color on the covers of popular magazines. It is made to appear as very desirable on the billboards across the country. Well dressed men and women are pictured serving and drinking it. In almost every television story the actors are seen drinking. Its popularity makes it a most dangerous drug. Young people accept it as the proper thing and do not see beyond the advertisements. They do not know that there is a side to the effects other than the one advertised. When a man gets a little liquor in his system, he loses his restraints and his will power. He becomes like an animal with no power to think and reason. He may look for a way to satisfy his lusts.

Drunkenness, in itself, is enough to destroy a home. A man may become quarrelsome and abusive under the influence of alcohol and bring unbearable hardships on his family. I have very little sympathy for any young lady who marries a man who is a drunkard. Perhaps I should change my feelings and say that I have great sympathy for a young lady who has to pay such a price for her folly. Young people, because they are young and inexperienced, often make very unwise decisions, but any one who deliberately marries a man who has the drink habit will certainly pay an enormous price for her foolishness. Thousands of homes have been destroyed, and wives and children have been left in poverty and misery thereby. Young lady, if you do not want to spend a lifetime with a drunkard, do not marry one. God did not give drunkenness as a cause which would allow a woman to divorce her husband. Living with such a man may be dangerous and intolerable, but she cannot lawfully put him away. There is no way of estimating how many such marriages have ended in divorce and how many others are miserable and depraved. The money that should be spent on clothing and food may go for liquor, and the family is made to suffer. Not only do they suffer for food and clothing but also for friends. They are looked down on, and the children may become social outcasts. If there were some way to clean the liquor out of the homes, there would be fewer divorces and evils of other kinds. It is in cities where alcohol is consumed in greatest quantities that divorces are most common. We might suggest our nation's capital and Hollywood as examples. The various other drugs that have gained the limelight in the news of recent years have played their part in destroying our homes. Young people, do not subject yourselves to mind-destroying, body-decaying, and home-wrecking drugs of any nature.

"But if ye bite and devour one another, take heed that ye be not consumed one of another." (Gal. 5:15.) This writer was writing to members of the church to plead for love for one another and for all to walk after the Spirit and not after the flesh. This would apply in the matter of fellowship within the body of Christ. Would it not apply in the home partnership? We have already mentioned that some men are irritable and abusive when they are drunk and make their wives and children suffer. Some do not have to be drunk to be unreasonable, soon angry, selfish, demanding, and unkind. Other such like words could be added to describe a disposition that is arrogant and domineering. Men do not have a monopoly on this hateful disposition. Many women also possess it, and it always makes for unhappiness in the home.

The church in many localities has suffered from some self-willed man who gained the place of leadership and had his way or made a constant disturbance when he was crossed. Such a man would be expected to have the same attitudes in the home where he is the head and where his wife and children are due to be subject to him. He may exert his authority with such arrogance and force that his wife becomes either browbeaten to the point that she has no will of her own, or she may rebel against his unreasonable attitude and seek freedom from the ties that bind her.

Some young couples quarrel almost constantly before marriage when they are in the period of courtship. Their natures and personalities clash so that there is continual disagreement over both trivial and serious matters. Yet, there is physical attraction and lustful desires that hold them together. They need to be warned seriously by parents and friends that a wedding ceremony is not likely to solve the problems and make them suddenly congenial. Such marriages have little chance to survive and are often very short lived. A self-willed, domineering person may find himself alone in a few weeks.

The Bible deals with the sins of evil disposition as forcefully as it does with drunkenness or other sins that we think of as being so very grievous. Read such passages as 2 Corinthians 12:20, Galatians 5:20, and Colossians 3:8. It may be that we have not given enough attention to attitudes and dispositions when we look around us and wonder why so many homes break to pieces. There are some people who are so selfish, stubborn, overbearing and headstrong that their companions cannot live in the conditions that arise.

The Bible begs, "Let all bitterness, and wrath, and anger, and clamour, and evil speaking, be put away from you, with all malice: and be ye kind one to another, tender-hearted, forgiving one another, even as God for Christ's sake hath forgiven you." (Eph. 4:31,32.) Here we have both the negative and the positive traits listed in the two consecutive verses. Good homes and happy marriages are based on the good traits, while the unbearable marriages that end in broken homes or are threatened with failures are characterized by the evil traits.

Children in a home are blessed by the atmosphere of kindness, tenderness, and forgiveness. They are cursed by the mood of bitterness, wrath, anger, clamour, and evil speaking. In the first case they are secure and happy in the family unit. In the second case they are torn by being uprooted and tossed hither and yon from one parent to another when divorce has ended life under one roof.

More respect for the Bible can make for better attitudes in our personal lives and for warmer atmospheres in family life. "Better is a dinner of herbs where love is, than a stalled ox and hatred therewith." (Prov. 15:17.) "The contentions of a wife are a continual dropping." (Prov. 19:13b.) A continual dropping of water can finally wear away a stone. Many a good man has been brought to the brink of despair and often to divorce because of the continual nagging of his wife. His patience may be tried beyond his power to endure unless he has a strong faith that will cause him to turn the other cheek repeatedly and to set such a good example before her that eventually she may change her attitude and relieve his burden.

The dance is taken for granted in our day. I grew up in Murray, Kentucky, and attended Murray State College. It is now Murray State University. The college at the time I was there did not allow dancing on the campus. Naturally there was no dancing allowed in the high school or the elementary school. Can you imagine a situation like that? Is there a public school in our nation today where dancing of many types is not taught? People tell me very freely and without blushing that they do not see anything wrong with the dance. I believe that any normal boy or girl who has reached the ripe old age of fourteen or at most fifteen can see something wrong with it. Jesus said, "Whosoever looketh on a woman to lust after her hath committed adultery with her already in his heart." (Matt. 5:28.) Does the dance invite fornication? If so, it is a contributing factor in the sin of divorce.

So many of the songs that we hear on the radio and television are designed to minimize the seriousness of fornication. The lyrics are such as to create lust. The stories in popular magazines in many cases are of triangular affairs. This man is married to this woman but is in love with that woman. They are written so as to make the reader so sorry for the poor man who is married to the wrong woman, and to think how much happier he would be if he could get rid of this wife who does not understand him and could only marry the other woman. The television shows are filled with such stories. The private lives of the actors and actresses are centered around divorce and remarriage. Television is taking its toll on the morals of our young people. Drinking, dancing, vulgar talk, suggestive songs, and indecent attire are common on the shows that young people see in their own homes. Vulgar talk is one form of lasciviousness. It is very hard for a comedian to talk five minutes without telling a vulgar joke. The tongue can be a powerful influence for evil. "The tongue can no man tame; it is an unruly evil, full of deadly poison." (James 3:8.) Where there is less lascivious talk and fewer suggestive songs, there will be less fornication, and there will be fewer divorces.

Materialism has played its part in causing divorces. Putting the love for material things above the love for spiritual things has led many into evils of various kinds. When we speak of a "higher standard of living," we usually mean having expensive houses, cars, boats, vacation travel, and many other things that gain our attention on television and magazine advertisements. None of us is wishing that we could go back to the "good old days" of the depression in the decade of the thirties, but it is true that the extra flow of dollars has not brought a higher standard of living in the matter of morals.

Many women have not been able to live within the means provided by their husbands. They have been extravagant and selfish, and they have lost the love and respect of their husbands. Some men in such cases have remained with their wives until the children were old enough to begin earning for themselves, and then they have sought to be free from the pressure and nagging of their selfish companions. While these wives have been dependent on their husbands' salaries and have driven them relentlessly to earn more than they were capable, they have added to the unhappiness by constant complaining and comparisons of their lot with others around whom they considered more fortunate. Many homes have thus been torn with strife until they end in divorce.

On the other hand there are many women who are earning huge salaries in various fields of endeavor, and they, too, may be contributing to the increase in the number of divorces today. They are financially independent and their time at home is limited, so they do very little for their husbands and children. Thus, they fail to have the concern for their welfare that would be normal if they were with them more and dependent on them for support and companionship. The money made by such women opens the door to many temptations. They may join the child in the comic strip in asking, "Mommy, why did we get Daddy?" She feels no need for him, and she does not have the love for him that she would have if her whole life revolved around him. We love those for whom we do the most.

It is a matter of fairness to women to admit that through the ages many of them who were unhappy with their husbands and often mistreated by them had no choice but to remain with them because they could not support themselves. In this age, more of them are well trained in some skill which allows them to escape from unpleasant, arrogant, faultfinding, or abusive husbands. God's law is often forgotten in the intense desire for freedom, and children are made to suffer by the effects of a broken home. Often adjustments could and should be made. This world does not offer perfection, but forgiveness, kindness, the soft answer that turneth away wrath, and cultivated love could prevent the sin and heartbreaking effects of the divorce. If both husband and wife had the proper understanding of the relationship that should exist between them and a proper respect for God's law, such conditions could be avoided.

We have spent some time earlier in emphasizing the fact that a couple is not ready to marry if each is not ready and willing to leave his or her parents to build a new nest. "Therefore shall a man leave his father and his mother, and shall cleave unto his wife: and they shall be one flesh." (Gen. 2:24.) This thought is repeated in Matthew 19, Mark 10, and Ephesians 5. We have earlier looked at the principle only from the standpoint of the young people. There is another point of view which may do as much or more to cause unhappiness in the new home that has been formed, and it has caused the breakdown in many marriages. A parent, particularly a widowed mother, may make such a bitter lamentation over having her child, on whom she was leaning for companionship and sympathy, leave her that she may actually forbid him or her to marry. If the young son or daughter goes ahead and marries against the mother's protests, there is often such constant whining and complaining in telephone calls, letters, and visits that the parent begins to appear as a suffering martyr and the son or daughter as a heartless villian. Working conditions may demand that the couple move to a new location, and the mother may manifest the spirit of self-pity and wail, "Do you no longer love me that you are moving 'way over there? I gave you the very best years of my life, and now this is the way you repay me." Soon strife arises between the young husband and wife, and another marriage is threatened.

Parents are sinning against their children when they do not teach them carefully the law of God regarding marriage and help them in every way possible to build new homes that will be an honor to the parents and a blessing to society. Selfish parents who try to hold their children when the time has come to let them go are not acting the way God would have them act, and they cannot have the love that is due them from their children. The children will dread to go home for visits because they will expect criticism from the parents for their heartless leaving of them, and unpleasant conditions will arise there, if they have resolved to be true to the marriage partner in spite of all odds.

Why are there so many divorces? Because people have forgotten God and have lost respect for His word. They have become a law unto themselves. "In those days there was no king in Israel, but every man did that which was right in his own eyes." (Judges 17:6.) The morals of the people of Israel fell to a low ebb when they forgot God and created their own standards. God was their King then. He is our King now. When we recognize no divine King, we recognize no divine authority. The standards of people are determined by the authority which they recognize. If they have no respect for the God who gave the law of marriage they will have no regard for the law itself. When there can be a deeper faith in God and a greater respect for His law, then there will be fewer divorces.

"Therefore take heed to your spirit, and let none deal treacherously against the wife of his youth ... For the Lord, the God of Israel, saith that he hateth putting away." (Mal. 3:15-16a.) The Lord intended that there should be one man for one woman, and He intended that the two should be one flesh. He planned that the union continue until it is broken by death. He has not changed His principles from the days of the people of Israel. He still hates "putting away." He planned marriage for the happiness of mankind. Anything that breaks the bond brings sorrow in this life and threatens the very destiny of the soul. If and when there is a return to faith in God's way, there will be fewer divorces and happier homes.

Chapter 8

WHY DO WE LOSE OUR CHILDREN?

There are many parents across the nation whose hearts are burdened and broken over the loss of their children. I am not thinking of those who have lost sons in the war or sons and daughters to disease or accident. Our hearts go out to them in sympathy, but we are concerned with another kind of loss. We are thinking of children who are lost to the service of God. We are especially thinking of those whose parents are faithful in attendance when the church meets for worship and who are clean in their lives. These parents may cry in anguish and ask, "Why is our son not faithful to the Lord? Where did we go wrong with our daughter? Why have our children turned their backs on the Lord and do not worship any more?" We look at the parents and wonder with them. We may see them at every service of the church, and we observe their clean speech and their obvious interest in those around them. There are some questions that we cannot answer, and there are some problems we cannot solve; but we might find a few answers by looking more closely into the background of some of the cases.

In looking back, in many cases, I have learned that the parents who are so faithful now have not always been so. When the children were young and impressionable, the parents were also young. They were struggling first just to make ends meet and then to get ahead onto easy street financially. The father worked long hours, and the mother took a job to help out. They left the children with a relative or a hired sitter, and both worked to gain more money. The days off from the factory were times to catch up on needed sleep, or work on jobs around the house, or to spend in pleasure. The children were neglected. They may have had plenty of food, plenty of clothes, plenty of spending money, but they were neglected in the things that matter spiritually. They were not taught the value of worshiping and of studying God's word. The parents may have been nominal church members, but by their very examples they taught the children that worldly things were of more importance and certainly more desirable.

I am not intending to imply that those children who are taught very early in life are the only ones who become and remain faithful children of God. Fortunately there are many exceptions to that. That is the wonderful power of the gospel, that it can take one even in adulthood who has never known the story of Jesus and convert him into a Christian. I am dealing with the case of parents who are faithful in their mature years who were not interested in spiritual things when their children were young and easily impressed. They missed an opportunity that cannot be recaptured.

I went for a meeting some years ago to a little church where every member was very precious because there were so few. There was an elderly couple who drove in a long way to be at every service. Neither of them was in good health. The other members said they did not know how they would have made out without this fine couple. They were so faithful in attendance, so liberal in their contribution, and so loyal in trying to reach others. I learned that they had a large family of children, but I did not see any of them at the services. One day the man asked me to visit his son and told me where he worked. I went very eagerly to meet him because of the high regard I had come to have for his parents. I was given a very chilly reception. He was definitely not interested in the church or anything connected with it. I learned where the young man's sister lived and went to see her, hoping to talk with her. It was the same experience. She was completely indifferent to spiritual things.

I wondered and wondered how a couple so fine could have children so indifferent. Then I learned. When the children were very small the parents went regularly to worship, taking the family with them. One Sunday morning something came up in the services that offended the father. In anger, he took his family home and kept them there. He brought his children up as though they lived in a land where the church was unknown. He did not teach them the Bible because from it he would have learned things that condemned his actions, and he was angry. He taught them by his actions that the Bible was just another book and that the church was of no value.

When the youngest daughter grew up large enough to go on her own, she began attending with a neighbor. She became interested, not through her father's influence, but through the help of others, and she obeyed the gospel. She was able to reach her erring parents, and they were restored to faithful living. It was too late to reach the other children in the family. They had been too solidly grounded into believing that there was nothing but hypocrisy in religion. While the father had his children growing up around his feet, tender-hearted, easily taught, and easily guided, he had led them in the wrong paths. Now, I could tell him why he lost his children, but I did not need to. He knew, and he told me. He was reaping bitterly for his early mistake. He could not even discuss religion with his children. They would not listen. It did no good for him to confess his mistake to them. Their hearts were hardened. He and all others who make similar mistakes are to be pitied.

I wish it were possible to impress on young parents the seriousness of being negligent in their duty to the Lord and in failing to teach their children while they can be reached. Too often the young feel that there will be plenty of time later to think of spiritual things when the debts are paid and the children are older, but they are allowing precious opportunities to slip from their grasp. Later they may reach financial security, or their interest in pleasures may have waned, or they may have been sobered by circumstances until they are aroused to their duty. By that time the children may be as tall as their parents with outside interests and associations that will completely blind them to the things of a religious nature. The ancient people, we are told, had a work of art which represented opportunity as being a woman with her hair plaited and hanging down in front. This was to indicate that opportunity could be grasped as she was approaching but not after she had passed.

In the case we have mentioned, the father completely quit the church and kept his family at home. There is another situation that is almost as detrimental to the spiritual life of the children. The parents may attend when it is convenient, with a sort of lukewarm attitude, taking no real interest in the work of the church. If company comes, if they wish to go somewhere else, if it is a cold day, if it is raining, if they were up late last night, or if it is a good day for a picnic, they miss the worship. Such a spirit of lukewarmness is nauseating to the Lord. We have an example of His feeling when almost an entire church had drifted into lukewarmness. He said concerning it: "I know thy works, that thou art neither cold nor hot: I would thou wert cold or hot. So then because thou art lukewarm, and neither cold nor hot, I will spue thee out of my mouth." (Rev. 3:15,16.) The Lord seemingly had rather have a person's active opposition than his half-hearted, lukewarm service. It is very rare to see the children of such parents become faithful, active members of the church. They have been taught by actions that speak louder than words that the church is of no value, that it is not worth putting forth any effort for or surmounting the least difficulty to take part in its service.

When the children reach the age of accountability they are responsible for their own actions, and they will be judged as individuals regardless of what they were or were not taught at home; but it is hard for them to recognize this fact if they have been brought up in an attitude of indifference and lukewarmness. The attitude is contagious, and parents should wake up before their golden opportunities have passed. Even later in life, if they themselves become fervent in their zeal for the Lord, they may find it too late to reach their children.

There are parents who attend every service of the church and would not dream of missing who never tell their children Bible stories. By their public actions they appear to be devout Christians, but they do not study and do not teach their children. In this case the children may learn enough within the walls of the meeting house to arouse an interest in the Bible so that they will study for themselves, but there is danger. Just as lukewarmness is contagious, just so is the bad habit of not studying in the home. When there is no encouragement by the parents, few children will study. Then their interest soon shifts to other things which crowd out the lessons taught in the assemblies.

There are parents who attend part or even most of the church services and outwardly appear to be pious and faithful whose lives through the week are not clean and above reproach. I have always found it hard to understand how any one could pose as one sort of person and really be another. There is a word that we often overwork, but it fits here. Such a person is a hypocrite. He would like to appear, and often does, to good people to be like them and to be accepted among the faithful members of the church. The elders of the church may be deceived by his appearance, but God will not be. Furthermore, the children in his home will not be. Hypocrisy is one of the easiest traits for a child to detect. He knows whether his father is the same man on Tuesday night that he is on Sunday morning. If he is the same, and if he is a faithful child of God, the example he sets can have a powerful influence for good on his child; but if he is not the same, his influence will be just as powerful for evil on the child.

One reason parents lose their children is because they play the hypocrite before them. Their religion does not govern their own lives, and they win the disgust of their children by their pretense. There must be a direct connection between the religion a man professes and the moral life he practices. Morality is not all of the religion of Christ, but true religion will manifest itself in pure morals. A man advertises to his children that he is not a genuine Christian if he is vulgar or blasphemous in his speech and dishonest in his work. If there is beer or liquor in the refrigerator, the children know it. The child may be too young to write an essay on the hypocrisy of his parents, but he certainly recognizes it when he sees it. If his father bows his head and leads the prayer in the assembly, the child may be conscious that that is out of keeping with the words he hears from him at home. He loses respect for his father and for the God whom he claims to worship.

The religion of Christ is a taught religion. It is not inherited. It is possible for a child to grow to manhood in the home of parents who claim to be Christians and never understand the plan of salvation. It is no wonder that he is lost. He was never made to understand what religion was all about. His parents did not teach him at home, and very little was taught in the classes he attended on Sunday morning and Wednesday night. He was not told the Bible stories at home, and he was not told enough in the public classes. He is lost to the religion of the Lord because he was never taught it. Whose fault is it? It becomes his own fault when he reaches the age of accountability before God. It is the fault of his parents who did not teach him "from a child the sacred scriptures." It is the fault of every teacher in whose classes he sat in the meeting house. It is the fault of the elders of the church who were not watchful enough to know whether there were capable teachers in the classes. It is the fault of preachers who stood before him in the pulpit week after week with the opportunity to impart much knowledge to him.

A young lady who has attended services with her parents from babyhood may marry a young man who does not respect the church, and in three months time she may quit the church and join a denomination with her husband. The parents may grieve and cry, "Why? I can't understand what happened. Where did we go wrong?" Now, the marvel may be that every other child in the family did not do the same thing. She may never have understood that "there is one body." She may never have been told that the Bible describes a pattern of worship for that one body. She may never have seen that there is salvation in no other name except that of Christ, that "there is none other name under heaven given among men, whereby we must be saved." (Acts 4:12.) It is hard to change even a young person who has been rooted, grounded, and well established in the faith.

In imparting the knowledge that will cause one to be rooted and grounded in the faith, reverence for God must also be taught. I taught daily Bible classes in private schools for a number of years. In those years I have seen mischievous boys who turned into fine men, but I have never seen a boy who lacked reverence turn into anything other than a disappointment to his parents, his friends, or any one else. A boy who lacks reverence is rotten at the core. He is like an apple that may look good on the outside but is easily crushed in the hand because it is rotten inside. A healthy looking tree may be blown down by a wind that left others around it standing. On looking closely it may be discovered that it was rotten at the heart. Irreverence toward God and toward His word will cause the spiritual and moral downfall of any young person in the land. Parents must strive with every ounce of their ability to impart a deep and abiding reverence in their children.

We do not want to lose our children. The church would grow from the inside if all the members could save their own children. Too often they take for granted that their children will be faithful, but there must be constant watching and teaching. Satan is not asleep. He is an adversary, and he goeth about as a roaring lion seeking whom he may devour. (1 Pet. 5:8.) One generation does not inherit its knowledge from the generation that goes before it. The children of Israel who were with Moses in the wilderness and who went into the land of Canaan with Joshua must have been the most devout and best taught of all the Israelites in their history. They were faithful to God during the lifetime of Joshua and of the elders that outlived Joshua, and then, the Bible says, "And all that generation was gathered to their fathers: and there arose another generation after them, which knew not the Lord, nor yet the works which he had done for Israel." We should not be surprised that the very next statement made about them is, "And the children of Israel did evil in the sight of the Lord and served Baalim: and they forsook the Lord God of their fathers, which brought them out of the land of Egypt, and followed other gods, of the gods of the people that were round about them, and bowed themselves unto them, and provoked the Lord to jealousy." (Judges 2:10-12.) Although the people of one generation were so very faithful, they failed to do what Moses begged them repeatedly to do when he made the speeches near the close of his life as recorded in the book of Deuteronomy. They did not teach the word of God which they had learned to their sons and their sons' sons after them, and they allowed a generation to arise that "knew not God."

Why do we lose our children? I do not claim to know all the answers. Could one reason be that we are not careful enough of their associates? Do we allow them to be constantly in an environment that is detrimental to their faith? Much that parents may do in the home can be completely destroyed by their children's peers at school and especially in their social life after school. The primary explanation as to why so many children are lost to the church and even to moral decency is often that there has been a failure to advise against and shield from the wrong kind of companionship. Parents may teach a little, but the children do not stay with their parents all the time. They may spend much time with their worldly associates so that they become more like their companions than like their parents. This is no marvel. It is the natural thing. Paul wrote to the church at Corinth and said, "Be not deceived: evil communications corrupt good manners." (1 Cor. 15:33.) The American Standard Version says the same thing in more modern language. "Be not deceived: evil companionships corrupt good morals." Parents, keep your children in the right company if you would save them.

Let your home be an attractive gathering place. Use your God-given authority in refusing to allow your children to go to some places and be out with some people. Give your gracious and cheerful permission to them when they ask to go to good places with good companions. It is not hard to see that young people can be easily and greatly influenced by others their own age. A farmer may carefully prepare the soil, plant good seed, fertilize properly, cultivate regularly, and even irrigate, and yet he may lose the harvest to some little insect that he did not suspect. He must watch everything. Parents must also watch everything that might threaten the moral and spiritual welfare of their precious offspring.

The public school system grew out of a great American dream to provide free basic education to all classes of children. It was a great advancement in the culture of our nation. Before the free schools there were private schools supported by tuition. The private schools could maintain a better quality of pupils. They were not forced by law to accept all children, even the wild, untrained, unrestrained "natural brute beasts." They could include the Bible as the chief textbook, and they generally did. Education obtained under such situations was far better, but many parents were not able to pay the tuition. That meant that poor children, no matter how worthy, could not have an education. It was certainly a great and noble dream that public schools be provided so all children regardless of financial conditions could have basic training in reading, writing, and arithmetic. Many have been greatly blessed by the opportunities the public schools have afforded.

It is next to impossible to teach the Bible in the public schools now. Many have recognized the need, and efforts have been made to work out some satisfactory plans; but there are many pitfalls and mountains in the way. Some public school systems have used teachers who have been approved by the ministerial association and supported by "love offerings" from the parents rather than by tax money. Pupils were encouraged to take these courses, although generally they were not required. Such teachers would teach the emotional, "get religion," faith only type of religion. I would not want my grandchildren in such classes. It often turns out that the less that is said about the Bible the better because when it is discussed the wrong things are said.

Another plan that has been tried in a few public school systems is to allow any church in town that chooses to, to provide and support a qualified teacher for a credit course in Bible. In such cases pupils who want to take Bible may do so under the teacher of their choice. This is a far better plan. Several colleges have opened their doors to such an arrangement. I heartily approve it. A Christian who is teaching the course can speak the truth plainly. There is nothing that is more seriously needed than knowledge of and respect for the Bible. Even one good course in Bible in a typical American college would be like a ray of light in a dark place.

Much of the evolution, teachings on trial marriages, and other powerful destructive doctrines enter our society through the schools. Even Communists teach in some of our American universities, and they are atheists. In some cities the schools are scenes of riots and violence. Teaching in such schools becomes an occupation with great physical danger. Pupils are also in danger from the unruly conduct on the campus. Robbery, rapes, and thefts are common in our day. What I am saying may be considered as a cynical and unreal suggestion, but the public school system seems to be rushing toward a condition that will lead to its rejection by people for its failure. Especially will this be true if there should come a revival of interest in the Bible and in righteous and decent living. Since I am not an inspired prophet I shall drop the subject right here.

I worked hard for twenty years as a teacher in and as a founder of private elementary and high schools. We sought to make them adjuncts of the home and not of the church. In hundreds of public appearances the point was made that the school should keep its hands out of the church treasuries, because Christ is the head of the church and He has not authorized it to do any of its work through boards or central agencies. We tried to find Christians and only Christians to teach so that they would have the pupil's interests at heart and would teach boys and girls rather than just Math, Science, and English. Special effort was made to have a good music teacher who would emphasize reverence as he skillfully taught the young people to sing psalms, hymns, and spiritual songs. Training in this aspect of worship could be a blessing to each pupil and to each church where the pupils lived. The daily Bible classes and worship periods were to fill the minds with knowledge of and respect for the sacred writings. Do not Christians have a right to teach Bible in schools? Under what circumstances would it be wrong for them to teach it anywhere? My children and many others profited much from the good environment that they had in such schools.

It has been heartbreaking to see some of these schools seek to become adjuncts of the church. They seem to imply that they are superior to the church and that the church should become an auxiliary to raise money for the schools. Are they implying that the church should release its funds to them because they can make better use of them?

What choices are before Christian parents in the matter of schools? Surely there is some arrangement better than the irreligious tax supported public school system. The public school is primarily a modern arrangement, and it is proving itself to be very undesirable.

The physical education classes seem to be set on breaking down modesty and encouraging lust through the modern unholy dance. The junior-senior prom and many other special events are often lascivious in nature and may become occasions of drunkenness and fornication. The school sponsored events and lax parental authority often lead to soul-destroying conduct in rented motel rooms or parked cars after the young people scatter from the group activities.

I am frequently made to wonder if the parents and the school officials are deaf, dumb, blind, and ignorant of the actions of cheerleaders at the televised football games. Are the boys and girls normal? Do they have sex instincts? If so, there is no doubt that such instincts are highly stimulated by her balancing on his hands above his head or sitting on his shoulder and then falling into his arms. Such action could only be described as lasciviousness. They evidently have to practice repeatedly to be able to do all their acts. Is there a virgin among them? Do you ask why we lose our children? I may have found some of the answers. Too few parents are concerned with the moral behavior of their sons and daughters.

"Take heed what ye hear." (Mark 4:24.) "The tongue is a fire, a world of iniquity: so is the tongue among our members, that it defileth the whole body, and setteth on fire the course of nature; and it is set on fire of hell." (James 3:6.) If unholy words are set to something that is called music with a beat and rhythm that have been made popular in this generation, they can be very effective. Are you aware of the words, the message, the philosophy of life of many of the songs that are being shot like arrows into the ears of thousands of young people? Parents, you need to be aware of what your sons and daughters are hearing in their bedrooms over their radios and television sets. If the doctrines of the devil were taught in no other ways, the words that come over the air waves with that loud rhythmic noise would be enough to destroy much of your influence for righteousness that you think you are exerting on your children. Do not underestimate the wholesome influence of psalms, hymns, and spiritual songs which the Bible recommends. Do not underestimate the unholy influence of the vulgar music that is very popular in many homes. Even the instrumental accompaniment of the most degrading songs prepares the mind for the soul-destroying words.

The eye as well as the ear is directly connected with the mind. Television can and does use both avenues, seeing and hearing, to teach the philosophies that have wrecked the lives of most of the entertainers. Radio uses the one avenue of hearing, but it is also very effective in teaching the same philosophies. America is being entertained by violence, immodesty, vulgarity, fornication, evolution, liquor drinking, gambling, and general mockery of the righteousness of God. Radio and television could be powerful instruments for very worth-while teaching, for clean entertainment, and indoctrination of patriotism. Are they often put to such good use? If you pay no attention to the programs your children see and hear and offer no guidance as to what is good or bad, you may later be among the number that cries, "Why did we lose our children?" The networks must be under the direction of some of the devil's chief lieutenants. Beware! You are interested in the spiritual welfare of your children, are you not?

Many in America do not read very much. They do buy tens of thousands of picture magazines of the "Playboy" type. You and I do not need to buy one of them to know what it is like. It is well known from the comments we have heard, or from the pictures on the cover, or by the name it uses. Far too much of America's reading is of filth. Far too little is unto edification. Do you provide good music and good literature for your family, and do you encourage appreciation of the better things? If you do not, then let this be a suggestion that you think more of such things. Many things that are printed are shocking, and some of these indecent, vulgar magazines enter into the homes of "Christians." Many are sold by business men who claim to be Christians.

Do we lose our children because we have closed our eyes, and stopped our ears, and completely ignored them? When we are considering the question, we would all do well to look through our own houses and read the titles of the books and magazines that are on the shelves. We should look at the names of the records in the stacks, and listen to a few of the popular radio and television shows. We might be able to save some of our children by a good housecleaning.

Our affluence has taken the children out of the "living" room. They have rooms of their own with their own radio and television set. They have a "den" where they can visit and play games with their friends while the parents visit with theirs. Are we not glad to have them out of the way so that we are not disturbed and can better enjoy our adult friends? Then when there are no visitors, it is very relaxing in the evening after the day's work is done if we are not disturbed by the children's constant interruptions. They like things better when they can be separated from any one who might scold for disturbances. This generation has central heat and air conditioning that make the entire house comfortable, so there is not the grouping together for comfort's sake. We may need to stop and ask ourselves if these pleasant conveniences are doing some things that are not good. People are usually able to cope with poverty as well as or better than they can with affluence.

Children learn from adults. In the days of my childhood,

as others my age know, there was usually only one heated room in the house in winter. When adults visited, and neighbors did visit then, I was in the room to hear their conversations. I was supposed to be quiet so they could talk, but I heard all they said. I learned much from the experience, and I became acquainted with the adults of the community.

When our daughters were young we tried to see that they knew the people who visited us. Oh, of course, they had friends of their own and were free to visit and play with them, but they came in the living room when we had visitors and became acquainted with them. Visiting preachers have stayed in our home during gospel meetings, and our girls associated with them. When children are allowed or required to be part of the family unit, they profit greatly by their contact with adults.

The so-called generation gap may simply be an acquaintance gap. The young people and the adults do not know each other. There is a communication gap because neither knows what the other is interested in. Parents may not know their own children because they have had so little contact with them. They live under the same roof, but they rarely see one another. The father may have gone to work before the children are awake. The mother, having seen her husband off to work, may have gone back to bed to catch up on her sleep. Children, especially those in the teenage, may get themselves off to school without seeing either parent. After school there is ball practice, band practice, or other activities that keep them at the school building. There may be after school jobs that last until bedtime. The parents have things that tie them up in the evenings, so there is rarely, if ever, a chance for all members of the family to sit down to dinner together.

All the activities in which the parents and their children are engaged may be wholesome and perfectly proper, but there may be too many of them and they may so conflict with one another that there is no time for family life. The children have too many decisions to make on their own, and they too often leave spiritual matters out of their thoughts and plans.

As a preacher in protracted meetings in unfamiliar places, I may hardly see a teenaged child in any of the homes I visit. I miss them, and they miss me. In some cases, I think they have been taught that "having the preachers" is a duty that has to be performed by certain families in the church because it is expected of them. It is not an experience to be enjoyed because he will be so sober and may be expected to criticize the actions of young people who do not attend services regularly. They are glad to escape the ordeal of having to sit through a boring meal with him. This is such an unfortunate condition; and it reflects an unholy attitude on the part of the parents.

Let me hasten to say that I do not find that situation in every home I visit, but it does exist in far too many cases. There needs to be more family living. Being part of a family unit would encourage children to take their share of the home responsibilities and remain a part of society and the church. The fact that the living room is often so quiet may not be such a good sign if there are children in the other end of the house who are growing up in a world with only children in it. That is an abnormal situation. In this age of television, they are not even growing up in a world of their own making, but are living in a fantasy world of immorality and ungodliness.

Parents, be careful, lest you be among the number who one day will cry, "Why did we lose our children? What went wrong?" Could it be that you just did not ever get to know them? They are worth knowing, and your knowing their interests and ambitions might make the difference in their eternal destiny and yours.

Why do we lose our children? I do not know all the reasons. A greater realization of the possibility of losing them might awaken some parents. We may take too much for granted. The child is born at our house, he grows up at our house, and we may suppose that he will turn out all right because he is our child. It takes constant work, time, and concern. Let us all work together to help one another avoid the mistakes and the suffering that the mistakes bring.

Chapter 9

A CONTRAST BETWEEN TWO WOMEN

There are two very different types of women mentioned in the Bible. One of them the Lord would look upon with favor, and the other He would teach us to shun. One of them is an example of the kind of woman a godly wife and mother should be. The other is an example of an unholy, ungodly woman who would lead her followers into evil and destruction. We want to look at the two descriptions and try to profit by them in that we try to imitate every trait that is good and avoid every trait that is evil.

Let us look first at the evil woman who is vividly described by Solomon in the book of Proverbs. It is not a long chapter. Let us look at all of it. Solomon speaks as if he were talking to his own son, and encourages him to keep the commandments he had given and make good acquaintance with wisdom and understanding, "that they may keep thee from the strange woman, from the stranger which flattereth with her words. For at the window of my house I looked through my casement, and beheld among the simple ones, I discerned among the youths, a young man void of understanding, passing through the street near her corner, and he went the way to her house, in the twilight, in the evening, in the black and dark night: and, behold, there met him a woman with the attire of an harlot, and subtil of heart. (She is loud and stubborn; her feet abide not in her house: now she is without, now in the streets, and lieth in wait at every corner.) So she caught him, and kissed him, and with an impudent face said unto him, I have peace offerings with me: this day I have paid my vows. Therefore came I forth to meet thee, diligently to seek thy face, and I have found thee. I have decked my bed with coverings of tapestry, with carved works, with fine linen of Egypt. I have perfumed my bed with myrrh, aloes, and cinnamon. Come, let us take our fill of love until the morning: let us solace ourselves with love. For the good man is not at home, he is gone a long journey: he hath taken a bag of money with him, and will come home at the day appointed. With her much fair speech she caused him to yield, with the flattering of her lips she forced him. He goeth after her straightway, as an ox goeth to the slaughter, or as a fool to the correction of the stocks; till a dart strike through his liver; as a bird hasteth to the snare, and knoweth not that it is for his life. Hearken unto me now, O ye children, and attend to the words of my mouth. Let not thy heart decline to her ways, go not astray in her paths. For she hath cast down many wounded: yea, many strong men have been slain by her. Her house is the way to hell, going down to the chambers of death." (Proverbs 7.)

Is the speaker not talking particularly to young men in this chapter? I believe that they are the ones to whom it is most appropriate. There are lessons however to fathers as they train their sons to help them avoid falling into a snare. Of course, there are lessons also to the young women to help them avoid becoming like the woman who is described. There are lessons to older women, to the mothers and grandmothers who are blessed by having daughters and granddaughters, that they may realize that with the blessings come fearful responsibilities of teaching.

I would suggest first that the woman who is described as being such an unholy character was once an innocent little baby. She was just as innocent as was the little child whom Jesus set in the midst of his disciples and said, "Verily I say unto you, Except ye be converted, and become as little children, ye shall not enter into the kingdom of heaven." (Matt. 18:3.) She was just as pure as any of the children were on whom Jesus put His hands and said, "Of such is the kingdom of heaven." (Matt. 19:14.) Every little child is born in innocence.

We are going to contrast the woman of Proverbs 7 with the woman of Proverbs 31. I would like to remind those who read this that one of these women was just as pure and innocent as the other at birth. It was not a situation where one inherited evil and the other inherited good. It was not a matter of inheritance. It was something that happened later that made the difference, and the difference is so great that it is beyond words to describe.

The woman of Proverbs 7 was given to flattery. Whether it be a man or a woman who uses it, flattery is one of the most deadly weapons that the devil has in his whole bag of weapons. It can ruin just about any man who is exposed to it repeatedly. It can destroy even a gospel preacher. He may be told over and over, hundreds of times, that he is a great Bible student and possibly the greatest living preacher, and after a while he comes to believe it. He thinks he is sitting on a pedestal and cannot be questioned. He becomes above the common crowd, and he looks down on his brethren with disdain if any one dares to question his teaching. I believe if people speak flattery often enough even a mature gospel preacher may be led down to ruin just as one would lead the dumb ox down to the slaughter house. The man can be led into showing the wrong attitude, upholding false doctrines, and standing for false positions.

A young man may flatter a young lady by telling her how beautiful she is and what a wonderful personality she has and by declaring his love for her and telling her what a good man he could be with her always by his side. She may be led to marry him even if he is an ungodly reprobate. He can lead her blindly by flattery just as the dumb ox is led to the slaughter house. If a girl will not succumb to the wile of flattery, she is indeed a strong character and can scarcely be tempted to sin in any way.

"Say unto wisdom, Thou art my sister; and call understanding thy kinswoman: that they may keep thee from the strange woman, from the stranger which flattereth with her words." (vv. 4,5.) "With her much fair speech she caused him to yield, with the flattering of her lips she forced him." (v. 21.) This ungodly woman *forced* him to commit fornication, and the weapon she used was flattery, her much fair speech. A man, no matter who he is or how strong he is, needs to know that he is human and is subject to temptation. He needs to realize that he can be swayed by the strong influence of another person. Many a young man has become immoral through the powerful influence of a flattering woman. "Let not thy heart decline to her ways, go not astray in her paths. For she hath cast down many wounded: yea, many strong men have been slain by her. Her house is the way to hell, going down to the chambers of death." (vv. 25-27.) The writer says that there have been many, even some of them strong men, that had come under her influence, and she had "slain" them all. She had brought all of them to the brink of destruction.

"For at the window of my house I looked through my casement, and beheld among the simple ones, a young man void of understanding, passing through the street near her corner; and he went the way to her house." (vv. 6-8.) It was a very foolish thing for him ever to go there. He was simple, and he was void of understanding. There is a short sentence in the New Testament, having only two words in it. It says, "Flee fornication." (1 Cor. 6:18.) That means run from it. There are times when it is not cowardly to run. It is the sensible and right thing to do. Joseph ran from Potiphar's wife. For a man to go to her door and knock showed that he was void of understanding.

Whether Solomon had a certain young man and a certain unholy woman in mind, I do not know, but to see even a strange young man go to such a house where the reputation of the woman was known would be enough to mark him as a man who lacked judgment. He had certainly not called wisdom his sister or understanding his kinswoman. He had not called on them to shield him from the deadly influence of this unholy woman. You could write the rest of the story if you knew that he went into that house. She forced him, but he went in, in a sense inviting the temptation. That is not what can be called fleeing fornication. Many a person has been led in the same path. A young lady who had worthy plans to keep herself pure has been defiled by the flattering tongue of an evil man. A young man who had been leading an exemplary life has been blocked in his efforts to do right by a woman who flattered him and who was loud and determined.

"There met him a woman with the attire of an harlot." (v. 10.) How was she dressed? The writer does not describe her clothing. He does not say if she were scantily dressed so as to expose her body and thus invite lust, or if she wore a certain color that would identify her character in that age. He did not say, but she was so dressed that when she opened the door, any one who saw her could recognize her immediately as being a harlot. He did not have to know the young man to know that he was headed for ruin when he saw him go into the house of a woman dressed as this woman was. The woman identified herself by the clothing she wore. She was dressed in the attire of a harlot. The clothing a woman wears tells a great deal about her character. A woman advertises her character as she walks down the street. Now, in modern times, I believe there have been young ladies who have been very indiscreet in their manner of dress and have walked down the street dressed in the attire of a harlot when they were not harlots, but their attire was contradictory to the character they wished to maintain. The clothing was an invitation to lust. If Bathsheba had gone inside the house and closed her drapes, the good man David might never have fallen in such a shameful way that gave the enemies of the Lord occasion to blaspheme and brought death and suffering to others. Aged women are to teach the younger women to be discreet and chaste. (Tit. 3:5.) Young ladies need to be told that they can advertise their character by the clothing they wear and that there is such a thing as the "attire of a harlot." Women are instructed to have modesty, shamefacedness, and sobriety.

In the book of Genesis (Ch. 38) we have the record of Judah, one of the sons of Jacob, and his sin of fornication with Tamar, his own daughter-in-law. Two of his sons had been married to her, but they had been killed by the Lord because of their wickedness. Judah told Tamar to remain a widow in her father's house until the youngest son Shelah should be grown up to marry her. She did as she was told, but when Shelah was grown up she was not given to him to wife. She put off her widow's clothes, dressed herself as a harlot, and sat in the way where Judah would see her. When he came where she was, he did not recognize her but thought that she was a harlot "because she had covered her face." Judah went in to her and committed fornication with her. His only reason for thinking that she was a harlot was because she was dressed like one. Clothing advertises one's character. The kind of clothing a woman would wear in one age to be dressed like a harlot would not be the same as in another age. Tamar was fully covered, even her face, but in some way she showed by her attire that she was a harlot. Mothers need to think more about the clothing they buy for their daughters to wear.

I was told recently of a mother who had suggested to her daughters that in order for them to attract boys they would have to raise their hemlines. The finest young men would be embarrassed to know that such attempts had been made to win their attention, but even the finest, most timid of them would be tempted when they looked at the girls. A mother is lacking in good common sense as well as in purity herself who would suggest that her daughters attract men in lustful ways. It would be the weak and unholy men who would yield to such temptation, and a happy marriage is not likely to result when two people are attracted through lust. If the mother is looking for some young man whom her daughter can trust and who will make her happy, she had better teach her modesty, chastity, and decency.

How would a harlot dress in our day? Where would she go to advertise her character? "Her feet abide not in her house. Now she is without, now in the streets, and lieth in wait at every corner." (vv. 11,12.) She picks the place where many people will pass by. At the corner there are two streets which meet. That is a good place to be seen. She likes the corner drug store where there is a fountain and where young people gather. Now, I do not mean to imply that it is sinful for a corner drug store to have a fountain or that it is always an ungodly place, but if it is a gathering place for the wild rebels of the town it is not a safe place for your daughter.

This woman who is described in Proverbs 7 knew how to win the kind of man she wanted. Two of the weapons she used were flattery and suggestive attire. A young man who is caught by her wiles is pictured as being like an ox that is being led down to the slaughter house, walking along with no thought of where the road leads. He is like a bird which flits lightly through the air not knowing that it is flying straight into a snare. He is like a man who has been arrested and is going down to have his feet put into the stocks of correction. He may know where he is going, but he is powerless to prevent it. A young man who is tempted by a woman may subconsciously know where the road leads, but he has allowed his passions to be aroused to such an extent that he has no power to turn back. He is being led as though blindly past the point of no return. He loses control over his senses and cannot resist.

Your son, parents, needs to be told often of this danger. Solomon was speaking to a young man. Your son needs to be told, "Son, don't go that way. Her house is the way to hell. Her road leads to spiritual death. Beware of such. Don't be taken in by flattery. Don't be tempted by lustful attire."

This woman was "subtil of heart," and "she is loud and stubborn." (vv. 10,11.) She was cunning and crafty. In speaking of false teachers, Paul described their "cunning craftiness." (Eph. 4:14.) Sometimes this world is wiser in its day and shrewder than members of the church. There are times when the immoral man is very cunning and crafty, and he has given a lot of thought to his trade. The immoral woman has the same traits. She was loud and stubborn. Do you remember that the woman who is of great price in the sight of the Lord has the "ornament of a meek and quiet spirit"? (1 Peter 3:4.) One woman is quiet. The other is loud. I believe I know the meaning of those words, and I believe I know the difference in the women they describe.

I know an older preacher who, in his early years of preaching, did a lot of traveling by train, which was the comfortable form of public transportation of the time. He necessarily spent a good deal of time in waiting rooms in various stations across the land. He often entertained himself while waiting by observing the people who came and went through the station, and he wrote down brief comments about them as they impressed him by their dress, their walk, or their behavior. Sometimes he would write a complimentary statement; sometimes he would make a criticism. Sometimes he would observe a young woman and write the one sentence: "She wants to be seen." Could you go ahead and write a description of her?

Now, there are some good, holy women who talk loudly, who laugh loudly, and yet we would all admire their good traits of character. They, by nature, are noisy, but I think even they need to cultivate a quiet demeanor in public lest they give the wrong impression to strangers who meet them.

When the young man came to the door of this "strange woman," "she caught him and kissed him." (vv. 5,13.) The Bible speaks of a kiss that is called a "holy kiss." I do not question there being a place for the holy kiss. I think

the very best medicine a child can be given when he has
fallen down and skinned his knee is a kiss and a big hug.
Husbands and wives should show their affection with the
kiss. There is a place for it. I remember so very well, when
I was teaching in a small high school where we had board-
ing students, seeing one of the overgrown, awkward high
school boys greet his father with a hug and a kiss. It is a
pleasant thing to remember. That son loved his father and
was not ashamed to admit it. That kiss was pure and holy.

There is a kiss, the kind the strange woman used, that
is deadly. It, along with the fondling, handling, and
bodily contacts, leads from one step to another step on
into the final step of fornication. She caught him and
kissed him, pretending that she was expecting him and
that she had been searching for him because of her love for
him. I do not believe that it mattered to her who he was or
whether she had ever seen him before. He was a man, and
she wanted his attention.

She said, "I have peace offerings with me; this day have
I paid my vows." (v. 14.) She pretended to be very
religious. She had been to the temple and had offered her
sacrifices. She had worshipped, therefore she was not
guilty for the day no matter what she did. There are
people in our day who try to separate morality from spirituality, who think one can go through a form of worship
and live any kind of moral life he chooses and still be a
good citizen. We have already had occasion to refer to the
wife of our present president who publicly stated over
a national television network that she would condone pre-
marital sex for her daughter and stated that she thinks
there would be fewer divorces if there were more of such.
America accepts her as a very outstanding woman, and
she has many friends. Morality cannot be separated from
spirituality. One is not right before God if he does not worship faithfully, neither is he right if he does not lead a
pure, clean, wholesome moral life.

The pagan religion was such that there were priestesses
at the temple who committed acts of immorality with the
worshipers. One of the biggest problems in the early days
of the church was keeping down the sin of fornication
among those who had been converted from paganism. In
looking at almost every catalogue of sins mentioned in the
New Testament, we find the sin of fornication or adultery
mentioned first. In 1 Cor. 6:9,10 we read, "Know ye not

that the unrighteous shall not inherit the kingdom of God? Be not deceived: neither fornicators, nor idolators, nor adulterers, nor effeminate, nor abusers of themselves with mankind, nor thieves, nor covetous, nor drunkards, nor revilers, nor extortioners, shall inherit the kingdom of God." He mentioned fornication first, then idolators. Idolators were also fornicators. When the church went out into an idolatrous world, it went out into an immoral world. The church in America today is in an immoral world.

Too many homes in our day, even homes of members of the church, of leaders in the church, are being torn to pieces by fornication on the part of the husband or the wife or the son or the daughter. No person should say, "It could not happen to me." No one is immune from temptation. Flee fornication. Run from it.

"She hath cast down many wounded: yea, many strong men have been slain by her. Her house is the way to hell, going down to the chambers of death." (vv. 26,27.) She had caused the downfall of many young men, and not all of them were weaklings. Many were strong and would have said, "It can't happen to me." They were left with scars that they would wear in their hearts until death. On their records they are wounded. They are like the bird with a broken wing that will never fly as high again. Spiritually, they are killed. "Her house is the way to hell." It is only a stopping place on the road that leads to hell and spiritual death. What a description to hold before a young man to make him beware of the wiles of a sensual woman.

An entirely different type woman is described in the last chapter of Proverbs. Beginning with the tenth verse we read: "Who can find a virtuous woman? for her price is far above rubies. The heart of her husband doth safely trust in her, so that he shall have no need of spoil. She will do him good and not evil all the days of her life. She seeketh wool, and flax, and worketh willingly with her hands. She is like the merchants' ships; she bringeth her food from afar. She riseth also while it is yet night, and giveth meat to her household, and a portion to her maidens. She considereth a field, and buyeth it: with the fruit of her hands she planteth a vineyard. She girdeth her loins with strength, and strengtheneth her arms. She perceiveth that her merchandise is good: her candle goeth not out by night. She layeth her hands to the spindle, and her hands hold the distaff."

"She stretcheth out her hand to the poor; yea, she reacheth forth her hands to the needy. She is not afraid of the snow for her household: for all her household are clothed with scarlet. She maketh herself coverings of tapestry; her clothing is silk and purple. Her husband is known in the gates, when he sitteth among the elders of the land. She maketh fine linen, and selleth it; and delivereth girdles unto the merchant. Strength and honour are her clothing; and she shall rejoice in time to come.

"She openeth her mouth with wisdom; and in her tongue is the law of kindness. She looketh well to the ways of her household, and eateth not the bread of idleness. Her children arise up, and call her blessed; her husband also, and he praiseth her. Many daughters have done virtuously, but thou excellest them all. Favour is deceitful, and beauty is vain: but the woman that feareth the Lord, she shall be praised. Give her of the fruit of her hands; and let her own works praise her in the gates." (Prov. 31:10-31.)

In contrast with the "strange woman," this is a "virtuous woman" whose "price is far above rubies." (v. 10.) This is the kind of woman we have tried so earnestly to picture in earlier chapters, whom a young man is to seek when he looks for a life's companion. She is the one in whom her husband can safely trust and one who "will do him good and not evil all the days of her life." (vv. 11,12.) She is an asset and not a liability to him. She is never a millstone about his neck. Happy marriages are built on that kind of character. Her price is far above rubies. There is no way of measuring her worth. A man, every man who is worthy of her, needs that kind of wife.

The virtuous woman is industrious and looks well to the ways of her household. She is not idle, because only by diligence can she keep her household well fed and well clothed. She works willingly, never complaining about her lot in life. There are duties that a "keeper at home" must perform again and again, day after day, which could become monotonous and boring unless she loves her husband and her children and she works for them. The duties are means to an end. The end is pleasing her husband. She works willingly and pleasantly. She does her husband good. Through her efforts she has a well run house, rising up early in the morning to direct the affairs of the day. Laziness and idleness are two words that she does not know. She has maidens working for her, and there in the home they make things and sell them. There is nothing wrong with a woman's earning money, if she does not neglect her family in order to do her work.

This woman was benevolent. "She stretcheth out her hand to the poor; yea, she reacheth forth her hands to the needy." (v. 20.) We have already thought about a woman as a good neighbor, so we will merely refer to it here as a characteristic of this good woman. She would be one to whom one could turn in time of sickness or trouble of any kind and find help and comfort.

"She openeth her mouth with wisdom; and in her tongue is the law of kindness." (v. 26.) When she opened her mouth she had something to say that was worth hearing. She could guide the house, as a Christian woman is instructed to do (1 Tim. 5:14), if she is able patiently, wisely, and kindly to teach her children and direct them in the ways of the Lord. A mother who knows the stories of the Bible and begins very early in her children's lives to teach them will have rewards in years to come.

My wife's mother was left a widow with seven small children to raise in the days before Social Security. Only by a stern will and relentless effort was she able to keep her family together and eke out a living. She worked without pausing from early morning until late at night. My wife says that she cannot remember when she did not know the story of Joseph, or of Samson, of David, of Ruth, of Esther, of other Bible characters. She is one of the youngest of the children, and when she came along the stories had already been told repeatedly to the older children. In her cradle before she could understand words, she heard the stories. How did that busy woman find time to tell Bible stories to her children? Her days were filled with very hard, tiring work. How could she stop to talk with her children? Frankly, she did not stop. She had them by her side almost all of the time. She talked while she worked. She churned and told Bible stories. She darned socks and told stories. She hoed beans and told stories. The children were sometimes short of things that money could buy, but they were provided with food for both the body and the soul. "She opened her mouth with wisdom." There are ways of finding time to teach spiritual lessons to children regardless of how busy a parent is providing physical necessities.

What is a mother for? Is she just to cook, sew, wash, iron, and clean? Is she to say something? There are words to be said, words of instruction concerning both physical and spiritual things, words of praise for children's deeds that are well done, words of comfort over hurts children suffer, words of rebuke over misdeeds, and words of joy and delight over shared pleasures. A mother should be remembered because of things she says. The world is starving to death for words of kindness. Children starve for kindness and love.

"Her children rise up and call her blessed; her husband also, and he praiseth her. Many daughters have done virtuously, but thou excellest them all." (vv. 28,29.) What a lovely character she must have possessed to have such respect and praise from her husband and her children. I am reminded here of something that happened some years ago which illustrates the very opposite attitude that a child might have for his mother. I left my wife and two half grown daughters in the car one day while I ran into the post office for a few minutes. When I came back to the car, I found all three of them quite upset. A broad shouldered young man perhaps twenty one years of age or near that had come out of a cafe which adjoined the little post office. He was very angry. Right behind him was his mother, who owned the cafe. They were arguing very loudly. She said, "You can't have the car." He said, "I will have the car." When she continued to protest, he turned and with his open hand slapped her across the face. He went, got in the car, and drove away. What a dreadful thing to happen! It was a very bad reflection on that young man. Regardless of the lack of training he had had at home, he was old enough to be accountable for his own actions and should have learned somewhere along the way from some other source to show respect for his mother. There was a great deal of reflection on her, too, would you not say? Was she like the worthy woman of Proverbs 31? I do not think so. If she had been, her son would have respected her authority and would not have disobeyed. He would not have shown such ill temper and violence.

The virtuous woman was a faithful wife, a good mother, a kind neighbor, a willing worker, and a wise teacher. It is no wonder that she could take legitimate pride in the works of her own hands and have praise of the same. A woman of this type now is a blessing to her home, her

community, the church, and to all far and wide who know
her.

Chapter 10

"SEEK YE FIRST THE KINGDOM"

The sixth chapter of Matthew is a great treatise on the providence of God. He knows what things we have need of before we ask Him.

"Therefore I say unto you, Take no thought (In our modern language we would say, Be not anxious. IL.) for your life, what ye shall eat, or what ye shall drink; nor yet for your body, what ye shall put on. Is not the life more than meat, and the body than raiment? Behold, the fowls of the air: they sow not, neither do they reap, nor gather into barns; yet your heavenly Father feedeth them. Are ye not much better than they? Which of you by taking thought can add one cubit unto his stature? And why take ye thought for raiment? Consider the lilies of the field, how they grow; they toil not, neither do they spin: And yet I say unto you, That even Solomon in all his glory was not arrayed like one of these. Wherefore, if God so clothe the grass of the field, which today is, and tomorrow is cast into the oven, shall he not much more clothe you, O ye of little faith? Therefore take no thought, saying, What shall we eat? or, What shall we drink? or, Wherewithal shall we be clothed? (For after all these things do the Gentiles seek:) for your heavenly Father knoweth that ye have need of all these things. But seek ye first the kingdom of God, and his righteousness; and all these things shall be added unto you. Take therefore no thought for the morrow: for the morrow shall take thought for the things of itself. Sufficient unto the day is the evil thereof." (Matt. 6:25-34.)

We have spent a great deal of time in thinking of how

143

difficult it is to bring up godly children in a skeptical, vulgar world. We do live in a skeptical, vulgar world, but this age has no monopoly on skepticism and vulgarity. Every age since the world began has had its problems. It was possible in the days of Noah to bring up worthy sons. It was possible in the days the New Testament was being written to bring up young men like Timothy and Titus. It is possible now. It is being done now. There are some of the finest young people living now that have ever lived. They make a sharp contrast to the "natural brute beast" type of young people that we have mentioned so often. They are bright lights shining in a dark world.

Why is there so much difference? Why do some young people grow up to be godly men and women while others become blemishes and scars on society? It is a matter of training, environment, care, and concern. It is a fearful responsibility on the part of parents. Whatever the young people become, whether good or evil, is a reflection of either good or evil on the parents. How can they shoulder such a load? Remember that our heavenly Father knows what is needed. He encourages a man to work, to earn his bread by the sweat of his face, and to provide to the best of his ability those things that money, time, and concern can give. Then He encourages him not to worry. He encourages a man, every man, to "seek first the kingdom of God and his righteousness." It is very important that we all have a proper sense of values. Spiritual things which will endure have far more value than material things which soon perish, and when we learn that one lesson, other things will fall into place.

The decisions we make in regard to our children's welfare should be made with heaven and the judgment in mind and not with dollars and cents in mind. The South has been until very recent years a farming section. The North has been the industrial area. There would come years in the South when farm prices would drop, or when drought or floods would ruin crops, and the family would be in dire circumstances. Too often the farmer uprooted his family and moved to some industry in the North. At home in the South among his relatives and friends he had taken his wife and children to worship regularly. They moved, and everybody was strange. Their religion was left behind. It was too fragile to survive the move. The parents had not moved for religious reasons. They did not consider what a move would do to their children. They moved in order to have more money for more food and more clothing. They could accumulate nothing back at home with cotton eight cents a pound, but in a war time job perhaps in the North they could pay debts and put money in the bank. They left their religion in the South.

There were exceptions to that rule. There were very faithful families who were hard pressed financially who moved to better jobs and took their religion with them. There is not any Bible principle violated when a man has a chance for a better paying job and moves to it if he can remember the Lord in so doing. Many such men moved into areas where there was no church and started one in their own living rooms. They would advertise in the newspapers and on the job and find others who had moved there with whom they could worship. Numbers of churches have been started that very way.

There is always a danger to children in moving. Moves to different parts of the country can be an educational benefit to them and an enlarging of their horizons, but there are grave dangers as well. There will be new associates, and if there is no church in town, all those associates must of necessity be of the world. It is very important when parents plan a move to consider the spiritual welfare of their children. A man may be offered a promotion by his company which would mean an increase in salary. He would have to move away from the home town where his relatives live, where he has grown up, where he has started a family of his own. One of the first thoughts that should come to his mind is "What will this move do to my family's spiritual life?" Such thoughts are part of bringing up his children in the nurture and admonition of the Lord. It is part of seeking first the kingdom of God and His righteousness.

When a man has "obeyed from the heart that form of doctrine," when he has confessed, "I believe that Jesus Christ is the Son of God," when he has repented of his sins, and has been baptized into Christ for the remission of his sins, he has become a child of God, a citizen of His kingdom. He is no longer his own because he has been "bought with a price." He believes that God has "appointed a day in which he will judge the world in righteousness by that man whom he hath ordained." How then can he presume to make decisions for himself without thinking of the One who bought him with such a great price? How can he arrogantly turn his back on his Father and look to worldly instead of spiritual things for his family?

I remember being in a meeting in a church where the treasurer was a man whom I considered a very faithful and sincere man. Some time after that meeting I moved into the county and was preaching regularly for a church perhaps ten miles from the church where that man had been the treasurer. I heard that he had moved into the very community where I was preaching. I was delighted and told the brethren what a fine man he was and what an asset he would be in the new church. He did not show up at the services. I went to see him and his family. They had not gone back to the home place. They had not gone anywhere. His wife explained that she had not gotten a new hat since moving but was planning to get one soon and then they would be there. A new hat? Now, I think a woman should have her head covered in the worship, but she did not have that in mind. I doubt that she had any conviction in the matter. She had moved to a new place ten miles from home and she thought she could not dress properly to meet strangers. I do not know what the man's excuse was. I suppose he could not go without her, and he did not take the lead as the head of the wife and see that she went. He did not take the lead over his children and take them. The whole family turned their backs on the Lord.

Sometimes a family moves, and everybody is strange. They left their friends at the old home. They are very lonely. Mother cries, and the children cry. It is a strange town, a strange environment. They miss their friends, and they feel lost and alone. One of the best cures for their problem is to be at every service of a faithful church. To have friends, one must show himself friendly. To make the proper kind of new friends, one must go to the place where the right kind of people congregate. One reason to attend the churches, in addition to one's duty to God, is to meet the people. If any man has left his father, mother, brethren, and sisters even in the sense of moving a distance from them, he can receive more of the same to the extent of a hundred fold in a new place with others of "like precious faith," if he will look for them in the right places. No one need starve to death for friends in any place where there is a church.

In one town to which I went for a meeting, the church was very small and was meeting upstairs over a library. It was a comfortable place and adequate for the needs of the little group. I was told of two prominent business men in town who were members of the church. I went to see both of them, and they both gave me the same answer. They said that back in the home towns from which they had moved, the church was large and had a nice building. Then here in this town it was so small. One of them said he had joined the big church with his business associates and he was satisfied. Neither could see much difference in the various churches over town. Was there any difference? Did it make any difference where they attended? One of the churches taught that a man is saved by faith only. The church of the Lord teaches that one is saved by obeying all the will of God. Christ taught for one to "take heed lest he fall." At the denominational church the people who attended were being taught that if one were once saved he could not so sin as to be finally lost. At one place the congregation sang without instrumental musical accompaniment, singing and making melody in the heart. At another place they had mechanical instrumental music. Is there any difference? At one place they observed the Lord's Supper every first day of the week. At another place they might at best observe it at Easter and at Christmas. The name was different. The organization was different. The ways of raising money was different. At one place they had a hall set aside for what they called Fellowship. In it instead of singing, praying, and teaching, they played games and ate together. Is there any difference?

Did it really make any difference where the business men worshiped and where they took their children? They could not go to the upstairs room where a few saints of the Lord met regularly. They could not choose their associates from among that little group. Why? It was to their financial and social advantage otherwise, and they made their choices with no regard whatever to what the Lord had taught. When Jesus was on earth He was able to convince some that He was the Messiah, and they left all and followed Him. Even some of the chief rulers believed, "but because of the Pharisees they did not confess him, lest they should be put out of the synagogue: for they loved the praise of men more than the praise of God."

(John 12:42,43.) Too often men get their values confused and emphasize the wrong things in life.

A man could well afford to leave a big church and leave his home community and go into a place where there is no church at all or one that is weak and struggling. He could afford to take his family and move there just because he feels needed. There is something wonderful about feeling needed. If the children have been taught from their earliest childhood that the church is the family of God and that it is the most valuable institution in the world, and that each member, young and old, has a fearful responsibility to do his part in the church, the move can be a great benefit to them. They can make friends at school whom they may be able to influence in a good way. They can enjoy taking even one new friend to the gathering place of the little church if they have been taught not to be ashamed of meeting with a little group.

There are other decisions that a family must make regularly that affect their entire home life and their usefulness in the church and in the community. On Sunday morning they must decide whether they will get up and go to worship or whether they will sleep all morning. They must decide whether they will worship or whether they will play in the water all day. They must decide whether they will worship or whether they will visit relatives that day. Whatever their decisions are, they will affect their influence for years to come. Children who are brought up to think that they are free to choose their activities on Sunday morning, and other times when the church meets, somehow usually choose things that prevent their worshiping. If they are brought up to know that they are to be present when the doors of the meeting house open, and if they are carefully taught why they are to be there, then the habit will be firmly rooted in them, and it will be hard to break. The entire family can be a blessing to each other, to the church, and to the community in which they live.

Can you take your religion with you on vacation? When you plan your vacation, do you work out your itinerary so that you can be in a town where there is a faithful church at times of worship? Do you just look at a signboard outside a building and assume that the things taught inside are scriptural? Do you even think about the church when you plan your vacation? A great number of people cannot carry their religion with them. When they have the car loaded with all their bags, bathing suits, golf clubs, and fishing equipment there is no room for their religion. They leave it behind. Have you ever wondered how many people take a Bible with them on vacation? I am thinking of members of the church. Some man may lead singing and prayer at the home church. He may teach a class. Yet he can pack his bags and load his car and leave his Bible locked in the house behind him.

"Seek ye first the kingdom of God and his righteousness." Lean on the everlasting arms. Be assured that no matter where you are or what you are doing, God is watching you and judging you. He is not much interested in lukewarm religion or feigned faith. He likes the unfeigned faith and fervent love that would cause you to think of Him and make all your plans for work or play or worship with Him as the center of your life.

There are people who plan their vacations carefully. They learn well in advance what time the church plans a gospel meeting so that they will not be away at that time. They plan their trip so as to be at a place of worship for every service. They meet new people at the places they attend and form new friendships. They are punctual at all services and are careful to have their children in the proper classes. They feel welcome and enjoy the association of other Christians. Their worship periods are highlights of their vacation. The children get the impression that the church is of great value, and pleasure and rest must give way to worship. They see joy in meeting with new people to serve God. They decide that plans to meet whenever the saints gather must be the first thing to consider when making plans of any kind. That is a very worthwhile lesson to learn, and children who learn it early in life rarely forget it later.

Parents who fail to teach that all important lesson by word of mouth and by example are not vigilant. They are not worried about their adversary the devil, who, like a roaring lion, goeth about seeking whom he may devour. (1 Peter 5:8.) They are not walking circumspectly. They are not wise, but rather fools. (Eph. 5:15.) They are not looking around to see the overall effect of the decisions they are making.

In many homes when I go in as a visitor I see secular magazines of various kinds. I look around more, and I do not see one religious journal of any kind. There are elders

of the church who do not subscribe to any religious period-
ical that is put out by the brethren. They do not read what
is happening in churches over the land. They are not
watchful. They are showing a lack of concern for the souls
of the flock under them. They stay willfully ignorant of
problems that may be arising in churches in other sections
of the country, not being mindful of the fact that what
happens in one section will soon happen in another. I
found such elders as this in several churches in the years
when church support of institutions and entertainment
was just beginning to creep into the church. How could
they stop a practice from coming in if they did not know it
existed? They did not look beyond the meeting house
where they went regularly. They were moving along
peaceably, and they did not want to be warned against
something that they knew nothing about and could not
see any reason for learning. They allowed the churches
over which they had the oversight to drift into digression
and evil practices. They allowed a generation of young
people to grow up untaught on vital issues.

I went to talk with some elders in an area where I lived
at one time. They had been told that I did not believe in
caring for poor little orphans and in having schools where
the Bible could be taught. In the course of our long talk, I
learned that not one of them took a paper that was pub-
lished by our brethren. They said they had decided if they
would let those issues alone they would not bother the
church. That does not sound like vigilance to me. They
were willfully ignorant. I think it is an unfair charge to
make of the ostrich because I do not think he is that kind
of bird, but we have likely all heard that he buries his head
in the sand when he sees danger approaching. Those
elders were evidently burying their heads in the sand when
they refused to be informed on the issues that were divid-
ing churches from coast to coast.

If elders do not warn in classes and if they will not allow
preachers to warn from the pulpit, who is going to teach
the men and women in the pews? Will parents find out the
dangers for themselves because perhaps here and there is
one who will study? Can we hope they will learn and teach
their children so that they can save themselves from the
sinking ship, as it were, when the church is lost to the
truth?

In the home is an excellent place to study problems. A

son may be ready to leave for college. The parents need to talk with him carefully, building on the things they have been saying for eighteen or nineteen years to him. They need to tell him that he will likely have teachers who will say things that will wreck his faith if he is not on his guard. They may tell him that man evolved from a tiny one-celled creature, and that he is only a higher form of animal with an ancestor common with the ape. They may scoff at the Bible and say that prayer is of value only because it makes a person feel better. There is not really a divine Being who hears the prayer or who has power to answer it. They may tell him that Christ could not have been born of a virgin because such a birth would be a physical impossibility. They may tell him that there is no set of rules to guide people morally or spiritually, but each person must decide for himself what is right or wrong in any given situation. They may tell him that truth is relative and what is considered wrong at one time in one situation may be right and wholesome at another time in another situation. Will your son be able to keep his faith in God when he gets to college? Will he still respect the teaching of his parents and live by the rules they laid down for him early in life because they found them in the word of God? Will he be destroyed morally and spiritually because he was not well grounded in truth before he left home?

Will your religion move from place to place as you move in your work? Will it accompany you on vacation? Is it the first thing in your life? People worry and fret over the problems that arise day by day. They worry saying, "What shall we eat? or, What shall we drink: or, Wherewithal shall we be clothed? ... Your heavenly Father knoweth that ye have need of all these things." There is no need that comes to us but that He knows. Perhaps He allows some to arise to test our faith as He tested Abraham. Would He be able to say of you that now, after the test, He knows that you love Him more than you love your family or your work or your pleasures?

Little children need parents for many reasons, but so do young people who are approaching the time when they will be leaving the home. By that time they are building air castles and making plans of their own. It is not necessary or wise that the parents press down upon the children their own preference in all details of life. The children's talents and desires should be carefully considered. It is important that the children do some independent thinking because they will soon be the adults and be forced to make decisions for themselves. That does not mean that they cannot be helped and advised in making some of the major decisions that they are facing.

If they go to college or trade school after they finish high school, they can better their opportunity on the labor market very much. They will be competing with many who have the advanced training. The ideal situation is for the young men and women to be "good friends" to their parents so that they can feel free to discuss their plans for higher training. There are professions and skills that are honorable in themselves that have undesirable features. The pharmacist, for example, may have to work through both services on one Sunday in order to have off the next Sunday. As a beginning pharmacist he may be asked to work through both services every Sunday so that the store manager or owner may be off for the entire day. A father should see this problem and discuss it with his son if he is thinking of going into that profession. Many young men have been lost to the church when they finished their training and got their very first job. I am using this one honorable profession only as an example of one which has some disadvantages which would have to be recognized and handled in some way that will not destroy all time for worship. Many other jobs in various fields have similar problems. A young man may train to become very skilled in maintenance of complicated machinery that is kept in constant use through the week but may be idle on week ends. The young man may be pressured to work sixteen hours on Saturday and Sunday and then have light work through the week. If he is interested in his soul and in making a home where he can train his children properly, he will be defeated in the most important aspect of his life. The salary may be good, but there is more to life than money. Let young people, with the help of their parents, make decisions that will not hinder their seeking the kingdom of God first. It must not take second place.

There are big-name colleges that are old, large, heavily endowed, and yet expensive to attend. Fathers may feel that they want their sons and daughters to have the "best," so they sacrifice in order to send them to these schools with such prestige. The devil has almost complete control in many of these schools. Atheists, revolutionaries, and even Communists may be on the faculties. These "doctors" destroy the faith of thousands of young people every year. Faith may be weak in the young person in the beginning, so the skilled professors may be able by blasphemy and mockery toward things eternal to destroy faith in a very few weeks. Rebuilding that faith is almost impossible. Hearts become hardened, eyes become closed, and ears become dull of hearing. Sending young people to such schools is very much like casting them into a den of lions, figuratively speaking. Parents who consider the environment and quality of training above the name and prestige are wiser by far than those who are thinking of pride rather than religion. Please do not deliberately send your children into situations that will almost certainly destroy their faith and cause them to lose their souls.

Many families in our generation frequently send their children to summer camps for their vacations. There are some that are operated by Christians that do not have the unscriptural habit of asking churches to support them. If you send your children to camps, why do you not send them where children of good homes go and where the Bible is taught daily with reverence and godly fear? Would there be any advantage in sending them among the ungodly and immodest?

Young people may profit far more than the pay checks indicate from summer jobs. They can learn something about the art of earning, and they can have pride and delight in becoming more independent. When they have such jobs they need guidance in how they spend their money and help in seeing the need of a careful use of it. With proper guidance and with the development of a feeling of responsibility, the young man can do a great deal in bearing part of the financial load of the college days.

Here again Satan goes about seeking whom he may devour. What kind of environment will the job bring with it? Remember the effect of ungodly association. (1 Cor. 15:33.) Parents, you are needed in helping plan for the *right* jobs. Your children need your help to motivate, advise, and oversee their work when you have helped them find jobs of the right kind. Teach them the value of giving a full hour's work for a full hour's pay. Teach them to be workers who can be trusted.

The sort of advice needed in regard to schools, camps,

and jobs can be given by parents who talk much of the church and many other things with their children. The young are capable of seeing the need for friends who are righteous and work that will encourage rather than hinder faithfulness to the Lord. Well taught young people are very capable of sober thinking. They have the ability to understand, and their motives can be as pure as that of the parents. Let parents not be satisfied to have children who are not Christians.

When fathers and mothers who are Christians set out to seek the kingdom of God and His righteousness, they are not thinking of themselves alone. They seek to point each child toward the mark for the prize of the high calling that is in Christ Jesus. One child may be timid and reserved while another one is outgoing and friendly, but each has a soul that will never die. Each child belongs to his parents. One may be stubborn and hard to control while another is placid and easily led. One may be brilliant while another finds school work hard and boring. The stubborn child may become a man of strong conviction, and the one who is slow in school may become a master in work with his hands. There is room for all, and all can live profitable, honorable, acceptable lives if they are trained to seek first the kingdom.

God did not make us all alike, and He does not expect us all to fit into the same groove; but there is that spirit in each of us that returns to God who gave it when the body goes back to dust from whence it came. It is not fair to show special attention to that child who is more like the pattern you had imagined for him and neglect the one who does not fit in with your plan. Partiality is an ugly trait at any time and especially in home life. Each child has a right to have a knee where he can sit and talk in relaxed security with a father who obviously loves him. It is not fair to try to force every one into a certain social and academic mold. All do not fit the same pattern socially, mentally, and physically, but all can be taught to be Christians.

In actual life there are too many homes that divide the children between the parents. Jacob was Rebekah's son while Esau was Isaac's favorite. This partiality led to great heartaches. Both sons should have been loved equally by both parents. A neighbor once said to my wife, in the presence of her two sons, "This is my son, and that one belongs to his father. We have one son each." This old story of favoritism comes to light too often. Father, mother, and all the children should hold hands as one family unit working toward the same goal of trying to lay up treasures in heaven. Let us try to have good homes even in this wicked world.

We speak of seeking first the kingdom of God and of the responsibility of parents to train their children in the way they should go. We then look around us and we see or hear of some mother who says that she cannot attend worship because she has a child or two. She is afraid the child may get a disease of some kind by being in the crowd. On the other hand he might make some noise and disturb those around him. Perhaps he is at an age when he is very active, and the mother gets tired during the service while she cares for the perfectly normal, healthy child. The problem may be that he has not been in the service often enough to know what is expected of him, and all he needs may be just regular attendance for him to learn to sit more quietly and calmly. All these excuses sound very strange in the light of Bible teaching. It says that children are a heritage of the Lord. They are God's gifts to mankind. Would He send us something that would make it hard, impossible, or unpleasant for us to worship in the way He commanded? That does not sound consistent with His nature, and, of course, it is not.

A child is not to be used as an excuse for forsaking the assembly. He is rather an added important reason for being there every time the church meets. We all recognize that the infant does not understand the songs or the sermons, but the parents are fulfilling their obligations by being there. If they are always present, they are exercising a good influence on others around them and even on their small child before they realize that he is old enough to notice what is going on. While the parents are profiting by the truth they hear presented, the child is gradually learning how to behave in the assembly. At a very early age he may begin to "play church" at home when he is alone or with other small children. We cannot tell when he is first impressed for good by being at every service.

Children should not be carried to the services to play in sand boxes or with building blocks in the nursery. Those things belong in the home and the nursery school through the week. Some churches provide a nursery with an attendant during the hours of worship so that the parents may "drop" the children and be free to enjoy the service in peace and quietness. On the surface that may sound good. The auditorium would be quieter and the atmosphere more conducive to a good frame of mind. There would be no noise to distract those who are sitting near. Look back at the nursery. What benefit is there to the child in being there? When does he become old enough to "graduate" from the nursery to the auditorium? How will he feel about making the change? What about the attendant in charge? Is it right that she deliberately absent herself from the worship to play nursemaid or baby sitter? Does not the command to worship extend to her? On what grounds could she justify her absence? Could the Lord's Supper be carried to her there, and could she partake in the right spirit when she has to cope with several children during the moment of partaking? Could she partake at an evening service in the auditorium after having been in the building in the morning in the nursery, missing it then? In my humble opinion, there is no justification for a nursery to be used as I have described. There should be a comfortable place provided for a mother to carry a child who needs special attention or who is causing undue disturbance during the service. The needs being met and the proper attention being given, if at all possible, the child should be carried back into the auditorium.

All should offer sympathetic understanding to the young, inexperienced mother who is trying hard to care for her babe and keep him with her in a worship period. She wants that little one to learn reverence and respect for God as early as possible, and she wants him to learn how to act at a time of worship. She should leave the assembly very quickly if the child cries loudly enough to disturb, but she should return as soon as it is plausible to do so. Our prayers and congratulations go out to her as she teaches and disciplines her child in her effort to mold him into the pattern of a well behaved youth.

Many mothers, in their misguided zeal, feel that it is so important to start their children in Bible class that they will take them while they are still babes in arms. The mothers will miss a class that is designed for them and feel virtuous for taking their babies to class and staying with them because the babies are shy and will not stay without them. The mothers, in such cases, need to go to a class where they can learn lessons that they themselves need.

The children who are too young to stay in their own class without their mothers are too young to go to class. They need to sit in their mothers' laps while the parents are gaining knowledge that can be imparted to the children in the homes. I love children, and I believe in beginning their Bible training as early as they can understand words and continuing the training until the day of death even if that is at a very ripe old age. On the other hand, I do not believe in putting babies and their mothers in a class together in the church building where games are played with the infants, and the mothers visit together. At one place I knew there were so many mothers in the infants' class that the teacher could not get the attention of the children because of the talking among the mothers. They were catching up on all the news while they sat there together. In another place the teacher was so pleased at what she was accomplishing in class because she had some one-year-old babies who would pat their hands during songs she sang to them and bow their heads when she bowed her head in prayer. The teacher and all the mothers, in both cases, should have been in an adult class.

We are talking to people who have reached the age of accountability before God when we speak of putting the kingdom first. Infants do not understand. The parents should make every possible effort in study at home and in the church assemblies to prepare themselves to teach their children in the home. Then when the children reach the age when they can benefit from group study, they should regularly be in classes that are provided by the church. The studies in the home should supplement those in the classes, and parents and teachers should be in close touch to be sure that every lesson possible is put over to the child.

We talk often to parents who are not worshiping regularly, and we have them tell us, "We know we ought to get the children started to Sunday School." Now, the children should be in Bible classes whenever there are classes provided for them, but the parents who make such a statement should realize that they themselves should be in the services when the church meets. They are the ones who have the obligation to worship. The children are an added reason for their attending, but *they* should consider themselves. Surely the Lord would say to these adults, "O ye of little faith," if He were to talk to them in person.

They might be shocked by the things He would say when He noticed their indifference and heard them say that they know to do good and are not doing it. (Jas. 4:17.) It is difficult in these days of little faith, and the many things of a worldly nature that compete for time, to awaken such young adults to the importance of putting God's kingdom and His righteousness first in their lives.

In summing up the tendency of people generally to put material things and worldly things first in importance and to neglect spiritual things, we are reminded of an incident in Jesus' life when He went into the home of some friends in the little town of Bethany. Mary, Martha, and Lazarus lived in Bethany, and Jesus often went there to visit them.

"Now it came to pass, as they went, that he entered into a certain village: and a certain woman named Martha received him into her house. And she had a sister called Mary, which also sat at Jesus' feet, and heard his word. But Martha was cumbered about much serving, and came to him, and said, Lord, dost thou not care that my sister hath left me to serve alone? bid her therefore that she help me. And Jesus answered and said unto her, Martha, Martha, thou art careful and troubled about many things, but one thing is needful: and Mary hath chosen that good part, which shall not be taken away from her." (Luke 10:38-42.)

"But seek ye first the kingdom of God, and his righteousness; and all these things shall be added unto you." (Matt. 6:33.)

Chapter 11

THE PREACHER'S HOME

Why should there be a special chapter on the preacher's home? We might not be able to prove that there should be, but we might do well to think about it for a moment.

The preacher has some very special opportunities, and with special opportunities naturally come special responsibilities. He is ordinarily given more time to use in study of God's word so that he may be prepared to stand before a congregation week after week and preach the gospel. By virtue of the fact that he has time to study and is obligated to teach what he learns, he is expected to become a good student of the word and know what it says on various subjects that he must teach to others. In learning what the book says, he is naturally expected to apply it to his own life, and he is expected to be an example to those who hear him preach regularly.

Now, there is nothing expected by the Lord of the preacher, that I know of, that is not expected of every other Christian in the church in his manner of life, his conversation, or his relationships in his home, but we have singled him out for special notice because both the church and the world have a chance of observing his life more closely than that of other Christians. His influence may be more far reaching because his life is more public. The devil would delight to have him make serious mistakes in his personal life and in his home life so that he can bring a public reproach on the church.

If a preacher makes a failure in his marriage or in bringing up his children "in the nurture and admonition of the

Lord," this can do very much in destroying his influence for good. The man at the factory may hold his job and win special promotions if he is an excellent worker on the job, and his home life may be a failure. His promotions and his standing at the plant may not be especially upset if his children become problems to society and are children of the devil. His public life and his private life are not connected. The same cannot be said of the preacher. A man may live the life of a machinist for eight hours a day and then go home to a private life with his family for the other hours. A preacher who is sincerely dedicated to his work lives the life of a preacher twenty four hours a day and has little time that is not public concern. If he does not want to live that kind of life, there are other fields of work open to him.

If the preacher makes a failure either in his marriage or in properly training his children, he is often counted a failure in the pulpit or in other public work. He may have great ability as a teacher, and he may have a pleasant relationship with the brethren, but his home failure is always a scar on his influence.

These things are being noticed, not to add pain to any good man who has suffered because of failures which he could or could not have avoided, but rather to try to impress on young men who are beginning to preach the great responsibility that rests on them. Paul told the young preacher Timothy, "Be thou an example of the believers, in word, in conversation, in charity, in spirit, in faith, in purity." (1 Tim. 4:12.) The word translated "conversation" in the King James' Version is translated "manner of life" in the American Standard Version. The preacher's talk should be exemplary, but the meaning here includes more than his speech. It is his day by day conduct. The preacher, young or old, is to be an example to all believers and also to the world of unbelievers in his day by day manner of life. The world often judges the church by what they see in the preacher.

It is very easy to understand why a church would hesitate to invite a man to preach and work regularly with it who would bring with him a family of children who would advertise his failure as a father. The children quickly become known in the church and in the community by both the young and the older people as "the preacher's children." There will be many conversations about their be-

havior, and how they behave will reflect either good or bad
on the preacher. If the behavior is unbecoming, the devil
can use this unfortunate situation to his own advantage.

In the eyes of the world a preacher stands in much the
same strategic position of influence as the elders of the
church. The Bible recognizes the fact that an elder cannot
do the work assigned him if his family is not a worthy example to others in the church. In listing his qualifications
it is said that he must be "one who ruleth well his own
house, having his children in subjection with all gravity;
(for if a man know not how to rule his own house, how
shall he take care of the house of God?)" (1 Tim. 3:4,5.) He
is to have "faithful children not accused of riot or unruly."
(Titus 1:6.)

The preacher's children must be in behavior like those of
a faithful elder if he is going to be in a position to talk with
young people with whom he comes in contact who are in
danger of going wrong. How could he warn them if they
could point a finger of scorn at his children? Now, their
duty would be the same, and they would not be excused
because some one else's children were doing wrong, but it
would be hard to make them listen to one who has proven
himself a failure in training his own. How could he emphasize to parents their responsibilities to their children if he
has failed in meeting his? His words would likely fall on
deaf ears.

All of us should have the ability to feel for and share
with those who have had their hearts broken over children
who have gone astray. We are not thinking now of reasons
why such may have happened. We are here lamenting the
fact that it does happen at times in homes of preachers,
elders, and other Christians who are trying to live godly
lives and set good examples before the world. There are
only two masters that children (or adults) can serve. None
can serve both. There must be a choice made. Is it fair to
be unusually harsh with preachers or elders who lose their
children to the wrong spiritual master? They are human
and subject to the same mistakes that others make, and
they will be judged by the same rules that will judge
others. Elders are given the responsibility of feeding the
flock, and the preachers are commanded to "preach the
word." They must exercise "know how" in guiding their
own families before the flock can safely follow the elders or
the congregation can listen attentively to the words of the

preacher.

All the brethren will be judged by the same book that will be used in judging preachers, so let all of them look carefully in their own homes, and then they may look at the preacher's home. It is easier to see the faults of others than it is to see one's own faults. The Bible serves as a mirror into which each should look to see if he measures up to what he sees there. It may be too late for preachers who have grown children to correct the mistakes they made in bringing them up. This is meant to serve as a warning to the young preacher who has little children yet around his feet to look into the future and determine on the course he must follow to guarantee the success he hopes for when his children are grown. He should have a sense of fear and trembling as he thinks of himself, his children, and the church. "Be sober, be vigilant, because your adversary the devil, as a roaring lion, walketh about, seeking whom he may devour." (1 Pet. 5:8.)

In planning for his future, a worthy young man may have zeal and dedication in his determination to preach the gospel. He has dreams of a happy home and a place where he can render great service in the cause of the Lord. He cannot entertain for a moment the idea that he might make a failure in his marriage. That could never happen to him. He may study diligently, prepare himself to speak fluently, and become known for his great ability. He tries to develop a pleasant personality because he realizes the importance of making a good impression when he meets people to talk with them about their souls. All such efforts are very commendable, and more young men need to develop themselves in the determination to preach the gospel effectively.

Too many young men with good character and worthy motives have been defeated early in life because they have been sought and won by the wrong kind of young women. It may seem strange to think of such a thing, but if a young unmarried man goes into a community to preach, if he has special ability and wins the respect of all, some young woman who does not measure up to the standards he has set for himself may make a determined effort to attract his attention and win his affection. He may marry her out of sympathy, seemingly feeling that he can give her a better life than she had known before. Too often she proves to be a stone around his neck, and his usefulness as a gospel preacher is destroyed. Beware, young man. The devil is not asleep. He will defeat your efforts in any way that is possible.

Just as may happen in other men's lives, the preacher's wife may be selfish, demanding, and domineering. She may be jealous of the time he spends in study or in personal work. She may be extravagant and wasteful. She can hinder his work by thoughtlessness and idleness. She may become a gossip or talebearer and cause friction among the members. Many a young preacher has become discouraged because his work is not effective, and he may find it hard to be accepted at any place where he would like to preach. He often does not realize the reason for his failures.

Fortunately there is another side of that coin. Whereas there are wives who are hindrances to their husbands, there are many, many who are stanch supporters and pillars of strength. Behind the faithful gospel preachers who spend their lives in unselfish service in the work of the Lord may be found meek, quiet, gentle, sacrificing wives who hold up their hands and give them their undivided moral support. They keep the "homes fires burning" and make the home a place of rest and comfort to the weary preachers. They guide the house and bear more than their share of the rearing of the children so that their husbands may be spared to do more preaching. They deserve far more commendation than they usually receive, because few people know the sacrifices they have to make to be worthy helpmeets to their husbands.

The young preacher and his wife may be inclined to think that their children will naturally be genuine Christians as though faithful children come as a fringe benefit for their special work in the community. Thousands of preachers over the centuries have learned that this is not necessarily true. Preachers' children must have teaching as individuals just as other people's children must have. It takes the same teaching to produce the same results. They need discipline, love, time, concern, and proper surveillance that others need. The parents need to be conscious that their children may be watched more closely by others because they are expected to be examples. Any departure from the standards set by the community will be carefully observed and criticized. No child inherits Bible knowledge or patterns of behavior. Everything must be learned by precept or example. The preacher may lose his own while he is trying to save others.

A preacher who does the work that the Lord and his brethren expect of him has a busy schedule. Because of that, he may neglect to give a fair share of his time, thoughts, and patient consideration to his wife and children. He has to learn to proportion his time so that he neglects neither his work nor his family. Success in the Lord's work depends on how he spends his time in the living room as well as in the study.

He may be harsh and unkind to his children when he thinks that he is really being a kind, firm disciplinarian. He and his wife may have the unhappy conflict over how to administer discipline. One may be strict and the other lenient. One may be firm and the other permissive. The children very early learn to play one parent against the other. Only trouble comes in such cases. The wife may permit the children to go places and do things in her husband's absence which she knows he would not allow if he were at home. She not only shows a lack of subjection to him which the Bible commands, but she builds a spirit of disobedience and rebellion in the children. It is very unfortunate when there is a lack of harmony between the parents in their dealing with the children.

There are times when the conflict in discipline arises because the father is impatient and unkind to his family, and his wife makes an effort to shield her children from the harshness and unkindness of their father. It is a great pity that some who stand to proclaim the counsel of God do not hear and heed their own teaching.

Considering the lack of faith that has come to our nation and the breaking away from the principles of righteousness and godliness, it is amazing and encouraging to see the large number of young men who are preaching the gospel. It gives us new courage to continue the fight for moral and spiritual values in the home because that is the base from which these young preachers are launched. The devil is not asleep, and he will make every possible effort to destroy their faith or to entangle them in false doctrines or enmesh them in unhappy human relationships that will destroy their effectiveness. Some preachers are taking strict heed to the doctrines they are preaching, and their fine, faithful preacher-sons bear testimony to that fact.

In past generations those who publicly preached the

gospel were often beaten, imprisoned, or even killed. They had to suffer great hardships in order to stand for their convictions and teach others. In our own nation only one century ago gospel preachers were given almost no income for the support of their families. The preacher often rode horseback from one community to another, living off the generosity of the people to whom he preached. His wife and children who were left at home lived like a widow and orphans. They had to provide for themselves as though there were no man in the family, and they often suffered great privations. If the preacher taught the truth on the matter of giving, he was accused of preaching for money, and his lessons were resented. Brethren were slow waking up to their responsibilities of "laying by in store."

Times have changed, and preachers today receive as much as the average person in the church. They should be thankful and should use the income they receive to the very best advantage. They should guard carefully against going in debt beyond their ability to pay because they should set a good example before others of providing things honest in the sight of all men. The preacher has some expenses that many other members of the church may not have. He spends more for books, for travel, for dry cleaning, and various other things necessary for his work, but he should learn to live simply and be content.

There are many preachers' families who resent the "fish bowl" type of life that they are required to live. They feel that they have the right to the same privacy that others enjoy. Those who have such feelings are usually those who wish to do things that they know to be questionable and they do not wish them known. They should realize that they are always in the presence of God. He always knows what they are doing. If their lives cannot measure up to the standards that the brethren set for them, it is doubtful indeed that they would measure up to God's standards. A man who is not willing to pay the price and a family who is not willing to make whatever sacrifice necessary to help him be a good public servant of the Lord should look for another kind of life. It is not fair to a church to invite a man to work and preach in a community and then learn that he or his family falls short of its expectations. Of course, the church has obligations to be sure that it expects the right things, but if the elders are God-fearing, vigilant, and worthy men they have a right to expect the preacher and his family to live exemplary lives.

There are many rewards and joys that come to a preacher and his godly family. There are the spiritual rewards that every faithful Christian has the promise of receiving. Then there are rewards in this life which many do not realize. Preachers have the association of the best people on earth. Now, as they go from place to place talking with people generally about their spiritual condition, they meet many ungodly persons, but they are not their closest associates. Even such people ordinarily refrain from vile language or improper conduct in the presence of one who preaches. So, the preacher usually sees the better side of even the vilest reprobate. He does not have to hear and see as much evil as he knows exists in the world. His intimate friends are those who love the Lord. He has "a hundred fold now in this time, houses, and brethren, and sisters, and mothers, and children, and lands, with persecution," and he can have the hope of eternal life in the world to come. (Mark 10:30.) The preacher's life offers so much joy and so many blessings that there should be no room for self-pity or complaining.

As to every life, so to the preacher's, there are two sides. There are things to be enjoyed and things to be regretted. The preacher is often encouraged and discouraged. He is praised and criticized. He is welcomed and shunned. He is flattered and slandered. He is honored and despised. He is rewarded and persecuted. Such has always been true. There are two great dangers that result from the treatment that he receives. There is the danger in times of criticism and persecution that he may become frustrated and disappointed to the point of despair, and he may be ready to give up in defeat. On the other hand, in pleasant circumstances when he is receiving praise and flattery, he may become exalted in his own eyes, and his effectiveness may be marred by his egotism. The preacher's wife should serve as his stabilizer. His home should be the place where he can go to find relaxation, refreshment, and renewal of spirits. There he should find encouragement when he is discouraged. He should find a welcome when he has been shunned by those whom he has tried hard to teach. He should find praise when his defenses are weak, and comfort when he is distressed. On the other hand, when he has been praised, flattered, and petted by the crowd, he can find a leveling influence when he enters the home where his wife knows his every fault. She can quickly deflate his ego and help him look in the mirror, as it were, and see himself for what he really is. She can help him say to himself when he is unjustly criticized: "I am not that bad"; and when he is unduly honored: "I am not that good." She can help him keep his feet on the ground and his head level. Every preacher needs the understanding wife who completes his nature and is one with him in the great work of preaching the gospel of Christ.

Every man in every walk of life has the right to the kind of home that will offer him solace and rest at the end of the day, where there is a wife who knows all about him and loves him just the same, and where there are lovely children who rejoice to see him return to them after even a short absence. The earthly home should be a simple foretaste of that heavenly home where the redeemed of all the ages will find rest, peace, joy, and happiness throughout all eternity.

Chapter 12

WHEN YOU MARRY

Worthy fathers and mothers expect their little boys and girls to grow up and some day marry. If they are indeed worthy parents they hope that the wedding day can be a very happy time for each son and daughter and for all who love them. The marriage certificate which lists the names of the attendants and witnesses, along with the bride and the groom, can speak truly of Holy Matrimony.

What day in the year is more pleasant to remember than the marriage anniversary? Is it not the natural thing for two happy home makers, who have worked over the years to keep the home as God would have it, to delight to recall the blessed day when it all began? This pleasant delight is only for those who have proven a blessing to each other and to those around them, and who are worthy to have pleasant memories.

For the day of the wedding to be most happy, the bride and the groom must have full confidence in each other. They must share the same hopes and ideals. They must have the same beliefs and the same appreciation for good people. They must have the same precious faith that would cause them to have a legitimate hope that God will bless them as He joins them together as one.

One needs to pray for wisdom in choosing a lifetime companion. If this wisdom is used, and if the conscience is clear, it is easy to offer thanksgivings and make petitions as plans are being made for the happy day when the two hearts will beat as one. After the solemn vows are made and after the happy honeymoon is over, there will be time and reason for ten thousand prayers of thanksgiving for one another, and just as many petitions for wisdom to be what the other companion needs. The two may and should pray together, but it will be very proper for each one to slip off alone for secret prayers to God who hears in secret and rewards openly.

Is it not a wonderful occasion when God the Father in heaven sanctions, the parents approve, and neighbors rejoice because they think that something good has happened? The joy on such occasions is not reserved only for the two who are becoming one but for all who find it natural to feel tender love for them in their own hearts.

When young people are graduated from high school or college we speak of a commencement, as if they are beginning a new phase of their lives. Is a wedding ceremony a sort of commencement service? Is it not a beginning? The future is ahead, and the wedding ceremony is the beginning of a new life when two will walk together into that future in a new relationship. Some one has said that the future is now, but not all the future is yet with us. The past, no matter how wonderful, will not suffice for the future. The future is what you make it. Mistakes of the past may haunt you, but the future may, by love, patience, forgiveness, work, and faithfulness to the marriage law, be made bright and beautiful. The memory of a beautiful past may be forgotten or hidden by impatience, laziness, unfaithfulness, or a lack of love. The past is gone now, the present is passing fast, but the future may last for decades before death or sin breaks the tie that bound the two as one on that happy wedding day. Let us repeat and remember that the future is what you make it.

The anniversary of one's birth is a day to be remembered. The day of one's becoming a Christian is an occasion to recall. Let the day of marriage be a holy day that holds only pleasant memories for the years to come.

There are big events along the way of life, but most of life is made up of little things, like little deeds of kindness, thoughtful words of encouragement, and loving expressions of gratitude. If you would have the whole building of your life be beautiful, let every little nail be driven in very carefully so that it will strengthen the entire framework. The good carpenter knows that even one small piece of trim that is not cut to fit can mar the beauty of the whole room. Let every home maker know that every sharp word spoken, every important work neglected, and every evidence of a lack of gratitude for a kindness shown can mar the beauty of a relationship that should be beautiful and pure.

If one of the two marriage partners is ever made to be unhappy, the other will be unhappy, too. The two are one. If one becomes a blessing to the other, he will be blessed. The desired happiness is a by-product of proper and worthy concern for the companion. Happiness is found in doing something good for another. Happiness is giving rather than receiving. Jesus said, "It is more blessed to give than to receive." (Acts 20:35b.) There is no realm where this truth is more applicable than in the home relationship. Selfishness can take the beauty out of any life and out of any relationship.

A lack of honesty threatens the very foundation of the business and government of our country today. Deceitfulness and dishonesty can destroy the very possibility of a successful and happy home life. Each partner in a marriage should speak the truth to his or her companion. There should be nothing to tempt one to hunt for a suitable falsehood to cover up some fact of his life. The husband of the woman whose price is far above rubies can safely trust in her.

There is a time in the life of every person when others pay the bills, provide and prepare the food, and take care of the house and clothes. The little people who are spared these responsibilities do not remain little. They grow to the size of adults physically, and hopefully to the time of maturity when they can pay the bills, provide and prepare the food, and care for the house and clothes. It is a very fortunate thing if two who marry have had some experience in providing and seeing after these very things before the wedding day. They have then had a chance to learn that money does not grow on trees and that things do not just naturally fall into place. Work is a part of life. What would life be worth if there were nothing to do and if one were not needed for anything? The daily work to provide a living and the household chores should be counted as something other than drudgery.

Two who have learned that contentment is great gain may be happy with food, clothing, and the simple things of life. They may learn to live within their means and to know that they cannot buy everything that impulse suggests. On the other hand, they may be so lacking in their ability to use their earnings that they spend a lifetime struggling to pay debts for nothing that they can point to with satisfaction. It is evidently far more pleasant to have something of value to show for what they spend. It is an art to learn to buy the things that are needed and walk on by the things that are of no value. All money that is spent in riotous living is wasted. When the money is gone nothing is left but the dregs in the bottom of the cup.

The beautiful spirit of unselfishness can be demonstrated in the use of money and talents. Each can use what he has for the welfare and happiness of the one he loves. There is far more happiness for both companions if each lives for and gives to the other. Self can get too demanding on pay day, if great care is not exercised, while the mate who was chosen for life is forgotten. After children come to bless the home, they have a right to their share of time and money, and it should be the parents who see the needs and supply them. Neither the parents nor the children should pamper themselves or the others by buying useless things that will perish with the using. There is a place for things that are bought just for pleasure, but they should not take priority over the necessities. The family unit should learn to enjoy sharing and sharing alike.

Love calls for time. The young man usually has far less time for other things and other associates when he has found his true love whom he desires to marry. If the love continues on and on after the wedding day he will still be glad to have time to be with that one to whom he said "I do" before a gathering of witnesses and before God. Time is one of our most precious possessions, and we like to give the best we have to the one we love.

The wedding day, happy though it may be, calls for a shaping and reshaping of many relationships. Now the two belong to each other. Each has moved away from the nest of the parents and from complete dependence on them. They have started a nest of their own. There must be much freedom in planning for the future and for carrying out their plans or there will be trouble in the family. Each must cut the mother's apron strings to be free to be a full time companion to that marriage partner. If the two look to each other and are encouraged to do so by their parents, this happy freedom will allow them to seek advice from their parents whenever such is needed. Parents must learn to give such advice freely, but carefully, as one business man to another. Father and son are now in the same business of home making. The same is true of mother and daughter. The time of the big man and the little boy is gone, and now it is time for them to be man and man. Father and son are now two men who love and respect one another. There should be no need for bitter words about mother-in-law. Each marriage partner should have two mothers and two fathers. They should strive to delight all by the evidence of their own maturity and their ability to meet their own obligations and to make their own wise decisions.

Hope is an anchor to the soul, both sure and stedfast. (Heb. 6:19.) The ship must have its anchor even though it is often on the move and hardly aware that the anchor is on board. Young people are great at building air castles, and the noble youth has worthy dreams. There may never be foundations under some of these beautiful dreams, but he should never be ashamed that he had hopes of accomplishing some worthy task. Some dreams come true. As two begin life together, let them dream and plan together. Their dreams may be beyond their reach, but the dreams are noble. They determine the goals that they set before them, and they stimulate actions to reach them. Life without goal or purpose or direction is not worth living. It is like a ship at sea without a rudder. It must only drift with the wind. The young people should plan for great things and build beautiful air castles together. Who knows, they might turn into reality. It is certain that worthy goals will not be reached if they are not first planned. Circumstances and accidents make all decisions for those who have no hopes or purposes of their own.

It is wonderful for young people to build castles of hope in the air as they face the future, but they must be prepared for the shocking storms of reality. Some castles fade out into the distance and are lost in the mist of time. The winds of reality blow them away, and then the two are left with their feet on the ground. Life is not all just fanciful dreams. Sweat and toil come into the picture, and difficulties arise to stop them far short of the mark they had set for themselves. They should not be discouraged. They should learn from trials and develop patience, skill, and determination. When a new morning dawns they can set out with new plans of accomplishment for the new day.

They should let no day slip useless away, and then they may some day see foundations under many of those worthy dreams. Disappointments and heartaches should not be allowed to stop one short in his struggle to reach his goals.

Air castles should include rooms in them for others. There should be plans made for one's companion, for children, for other loved ones, for all who need help, and for the church. The young couple should seek first the approval of God and determine their goals with His counsel in mind. Except the Lord build a house, they labor in vain that build it. "Seek ye first the kingdom of God and his righteousness." They should never be ashamed to let others know that they delight to be workers together with God. The shameful greed, immorality, and strife that blanket the earth are the fall-out from dreams and plans that were made with no thought of God's will. He knows best, and all need the counsel of One with such depth of wisdom and knowledge. His love is as wonderful as His wisdom. All air castles should be built with the full realization that the eyes of the Lord are in every place, keeping watch over the evil and the good. People who ignore God live their lives in vain, and they will have regret throughout eternity. Such lives are worthless to those who lead them and to others.

Worthy dreams and plans are flexible. All may need to interrupt their journey to help the man who is half dead beside the road. Sickness may come to one or the other of the marriage partners. There go some of the dreams, but caring for that one who deserves so much love is just as worthy as any of the goals that had been set. One cannot be happy in life if he is too determined or stubborn to change his plans to fit into life's various situations. Plans are to be made and enjoyed, and if possible they are to be carried to wonderful completion. When they have been completed and goals have been reached, new plans must be made and new goals set so that life can be lived to the very fullest extent.

God has spoken unto us through His Son, and this message concerns the great salvation. (Heb. 1:1,2; 2:1-4.) The gospel is the power of God unto salvation. It is the word that is able to save the soul. (Rom. 1:16; Jas. 1:21.) There are many wonderful by-products which may be enjoyed by those who have carefully learned the way of salvation.

Every young couple who undertakes the great task of making a home together should realize that nothing can take the place of the Bible in their lives. One of the first habits that the young husband and wife should form is that of reading the Bible together regularly and prayerfully. God knows what we need, and His law which He has given to us is "for our good always." (Deut. 6:24.)

Not only should the young marriage partners make a habit of reading the Bible together, but they should talk about it and pray often together. The family that prays together stays together. They should meet regularly with the saints to worship God. Cares, pleasures, and riches should not be thorns to choke out their spiritual life, but they should stay in their proper place. When the young people move into the first place of their own to live, their Bible should have a special place, and that place is not on a shelf to gather dust. It is not to be used as a scrapbook to collect all the clippings, pictures, and mementos that chance to come their way. It is not to be used as a charm to ward off evil spirits or as a sort of crutch in time of distress. It is rather to be regarded in its true light as the word of God. It is the only guide given us for our journey to eternity, and without it we will certainly lose our way.

Before you marry, young people, be sure that you have chosen the right mate. Be sure that God sanctions your choice, and, if your parents are God-fearing, faithful Christians, that they also approve. They are interested in your welfare and your happiness. Make a firm resolution to be faithful to your marriage companion so long as you both live, and let nothing come between you that can break the holy ties that bind you. Resolve that you will have a good home even in the midst of a wicked world.

Chapter 13

PHYSICAL RELATIONSHIPS
TYPICAL OF SPIRITUAL RELATIONSHIPS

The Bible uses the physical relationships of the home to help us understand the spiritual relationships. In the Old Testament the people commonly prayed to the God of Abraham, of Isaac, and of Jacob. When our Saviour was here on earth, He taught His disciples to pray after this manner: "Our Father, which art in heaven." Christ came to make known to us His Father, to let us know that His Father is willing to be our Father also. We understand the word father. In the physical relationship, the word stands for love, security, and protection. I do not know how many times in both the Old and the New Testaments God is pictured as a Father. The New Testament emphasizes the thought more strongly than the Old. The very term shows His great love for us, for after all we are only His creatures. The Saviour told His disciples when they prayed that they could come as unto a father and say, "Our Father." That means that they could come boldly to the throne of grace for help in time of need.

In explaining how the Father responds to prayer, Jesus said, "Or what man is there of you, whom if his son ask bread, will he give him a stone? Or if he ask a fish, will he give him a serpent? If ye then, being evil, know how to give good gifts unto your children, how much more shall your Father which is in heaven give good things to them that ask him?" (Matt. 7:9-11.)

Our Saviour came as the "very effulgence of his glory." He said that He came to do the will of the Father, and one thing that He tried diligently to do was to let man know

175

that God is willing to be our Father. In the sermon on the mount in talking of food, shelter, and clothing, He said, "Your heavenly Father knoweth that ye have need of all these things." (Matt. 6:32.) Earlier He had said, "Your Father knoweth what things ye have need of, before ye ask him." (6:8.) "Your Father," what a wonderful relationship! Your Father knows, and His hand is not short that He cannot reach down to help. It is "in him that we live and move and have our being." (Acts 17:28.) "Every good and every perfect gift is from above, and cometh down from the Father of lights, with whom is no variableness, neither shadow of turning." (Jas. 1:17.) What is your relationship with God? Is He your Father?

In speaking to the Jews who were bitterly criticizing Him for His teaching, Jesus once said, "Ye are of your father the devil." (John 8:44a.) In the last day, it will be a terrible condition if we are of our father the devil. God would have us change our relationship with the devil, which every one in sin has, and let Him be our Father instead. Jesus told the Samaritan woman whom He met at Jacob's well at Sychar that the time was coming when the place of worship, whether Mt. Gerizim, Jerusalem, or anywhere else, would be of no significance. The important thing is whether one worships the Father "in spirit and in truth." He added, "For the Father seeketh such to worship him." (John 4:23.) Not only are we allowed to worship Him, but "the Father seeketh such to worship him."

There is another side to the picture. If God is our Father, then we are His children. There is a beautiful passage in 1 John 3:1 which I consider a very great blessing just to read: "Behold, what manner of love the Father hath bestowed on us, that we should be called the sons of God: therefore the world knoweth us not, because it knew him not. Beloved, now are we the sons of God, and it doth not yet appear what we shall be: but we know that, when he shall appear, we shall be like him; for we shall see him as he is. And every man that hath this hope in him purifieth himself, even as he is pure." Is there anything better than being a child of God? We are told that here in this life we do not know what we shall be like in heaven, but we shall be like Him. How we will look is of no importance, and do not let any one convince you that you will look the same there as you do now. We do not know because it has not been revealed, but we know that "we shall be like him, for

we shall see him as he is." That will be enough. We will
have a new house not made with hands, and we will be
with our Father. Our Father and His children will be
together. Having that kind of hope causes a man to purify
his life to be like the pure Father. The more nearly a man
resembles his Father in this life, the greater assurance he
has of living with Him in the next life.

We stated in another chapter that the one basic cause of
divorce and other sins in general is the breakdown of faith
in God and in His word. When people are taught in school,
in the newspaper, on the radio, and on television that they
are cousins to the ape and all sprang from a common
one-celled ancestor, they cease to believe that they are the
offspring of God. They are made to think that they are
only higher forms of animals, and they begin to act the
part. The loss of faith is the danger that is threatening to
destroy the very moral fiber of our nation. If there were
some way to put back the faith that would enable us to
pray, "Our Father which art in heaven" and to
understand that we have the right to say "Our Father,"
then there would be a quick change in the morals of our
country. Peter dared put it like this: "Be ye holy; for I am
holy. And if ye call on the Father, who without respect of
persons judgeth according to every man's work, pass the
time of your sojourning here in fear: forasmuch as ye know
that ye were not redeemed with corruptible things, as silver and gold, from your vain conversation received by tradition from your fathers; but with the precious blood of
Christ, as of a lamb without blemish and without spot."
(1 Peter 1:16-19.)

Now, we are to be holy because the Father is holy, and
we are to be as much like our heavenly Father as it is possible to be. In the very beginning, God said, "Let us make
man in our image, after our likeness." (Gen. 1:26a.) Man
has the power to have worthy motives, to remember, to
reason, to purpose, and to plan. He is not like the ape that
lives entirely by instinct. Rather he has a conscience that
can be void of offense. He can serve unselfishly, considering the needs of others, and he can act as if he is in the
image of his Father in heaven.

The word Father is a good word. I like to think of it as I
think of fathers here on the earth. The word "father" and
the word "son" belong together. God is our Father. We
are His sons. We do not deserve all that He has done to

make that possible, but He has reached down in grace, having loved the world so much that "he gave his only begotten Son, that whosoever believeth in him should not perish, but have everlasting life." (John 3:16.)

"The Spirit itself beareth witness with our spirit, that we are the children of God: and if children, then heirs; heirs of God, and joint heirs with Christ; if so be that we suffer with him, that we may be also glorified together. For I reckon that the sufferings of this present time are not worthy to be compared with the glory which shall be revealed in us." (Rom. 8:16-18.) We suffer with Christ whatever persecution or ridicule some one wants to heap upon us, and we remain faithful, looking to the day when we shall be glorified with Him. We are heirs of God and joint-heirs with Christ, as if He were our Brother. Our Father, our Brother. That thought ought to lift man out of the gutter and let him stand humbly with hope, as he considers the exceeding great and precious promises made by his Father. Heirs of God, joint-heirs with Christ.

"For ye are all the children of God by faith in Christ Jesus. For as many of you as have been baptized into Christ have put on Christ. There is neither Jew nor Greek, there is neither bond nor free, there is neither male nor female; for ye are all one in Christ Jesus. And if ye be Christ's, then are ye Abraham's seed, and heirs according to the promise." (Gal. 3:26-29.) That will bear much meditation. There are many verses in the New Testament that picture God as our Father and us as His children. As we think about them we should be made to rejoice and give thanks for the glorious privilege of being in His family. "For this cause I bow my knees unto the Father of our Lord Jesus Christ, of whom the whole family in heaven and earth is named, that he may grant you, according to the riches of his glory, to be strengthened with might by his Spirit in the inner man; that Christ may dwell in your hearts by faith; that ye, being rooted and grounded in love, may be able to comprehend with all saints what is the breadth, and length, and depth, and height; and to know the love of Christ, which passeth knowledge, that ye might be filled with all the fulness of God." (Eph. 3:14-19.) The whole family of God is named of Christ. The word "family" signifies a unit made up of parents and children. God is our Father. We are His children. We make up His family.

Paul uses the expression "house of God" in writing to Timothy. He said, "These things write I unto thee, hoping to come unto thee shortly: but if I tarry long, that thou mayest know how thou oughtest to behave thyself in the house of God, which is the church of the living God, the pillar and ground of the truth." (1 Tim. 3:14,15.) The word "house" is used in the New Testament primarily to refer to the family relationship, not the dwelling in which the family lives. The jailer and his house were baptized. Peter preached to Cornelius and his house. Lydia and her house received the word of God. Paul said that the house of God is the church of the living God. The meeting house is not the church. The church is the family, made up of children of God. Paul told Timothy that he hoped to see him soon, but he was writing the letter in case he were delayed. The letter would teach Timothy how he ought to behave himself as a member of the church, as a child in God's house. He was not instructing him on his behavior in the meeting house when the church came together for worship. He was telling him how he ought to behave himself seven days a week whether he was alone or with fellow Christians or with people of the world. Wherever he was at all times he was still in the house of God. He was still a child of God, a member of His family.

How should a child of God behave himself? Very much the same way that a child in the physical family should behave himself. He should honor, love, respect, and obey his father and express gratitude for the things done for him. Do we not owe our heavenly Father the same? We can learn many things concerning our responsibility to our Father in heaven from the things required of us in the physical family. The same general principles carry over from one family to the other, from our earthly family to our heavenly family in which God is our Father.

In speaking of Christ's taking on the form of man, the writer of Hebrews said of Him: "Wherefore in all things it behoved him to be made like unto his brethren, that he might be a merciful and faithful high priest in things pertaining to God, to make reconciliation for the sins of the people." (Heb. 2:17.) Christ suffered for His brethren. Are you one of Christ's brethren? Is there anything better that you could be?

Christ said, "In my Father's house are many mansions: if it were not so, I would have told you. I go to prepare a place for you. And if I go and prepare a place for you, I will come again, and receive you unto myself; that where I am, there ye may be also." (John 14:2,3.) The mansions are in the Father's house, and we have the blessed privilege of looking forward to sharing the glories of those mansions with God our Father and with Christ our Brother. If we have such hope as that, we should not go around crying with self pity if we do not have a big bank account or if our health is not as good as we wish. Life is like a vapor that appeareth for a little while and then vanisheth away. It is swifter than a weaver's shuttle. Young people cannot realize the swiftness of time, but as one begins to go down the hill on the other side he becomes very conscious of it. We are here for a brief time and then we are gone.

What is life here in comparison with eternity? Our minds cannot grasp the thought. It might help us a little as we think of eternity if we consider the universe in which we live. I heard a man speak once who was a great astronomer, a student of the heavenly bodies. He had a drawing of the universe, or his concept of it. He showed various galaxies with thousands of stars in each galaxy. He tried to picture himself at the edge of that universe. Let your mind go, if you can, to the rim of stars farthest away. How far is it to the farthest star, and what is beyond it? Light travels at the rate of 186,000 miles a second. It takes the light from certain stars several years to reach the earth. How far does space reach? Can you imagine its ending? Can you picture eternity? How long will it last?

The things of this life will perish with the using. Nothing that we see around us is eternal. Everything, even the earth itself, will pass away. Only those things which we lay up in heaven will last through eternity. Paul said, "I know whom I have believed, and am persuaded that he is able to keep that which I have committed unto him against that day." (2 Tim. 1:12b.) He did not have many treasures here, and nobody was made richer by his death, but he had his treasures laid up over there. Jesus suggested, "Lay not up for yourselves treasures upon earth, where moth and rust doth corrupt, and where thieves break through and steal: but lay up for yourselves treasures in heaven, where neither moth nor rust doth corrupt, and where thieves do not break through nor steal: for where your treasure is, there will your heart be also."

(Matt. 6:19-21.) Paul expressed the same thought in these words: "If ye then be risen with Christ, seek those things which are above, where Christ sitteth on the right hand of God. Set your affection on things above, not on things on the earth." (Col. 3:1,2.) It is a marvelous thought that we can be with Him in glory as an heir of God, a joint-heir with Christ, and live in the prepared mansions, having God as our Father and Christ as our Brother.

Success in business in this life may be good, but it matters little after all because the things for which we strive will quickly pass away. Making preparation for the life after death is of greater importance. We have a Brother who is our Advocate with the Father, and He is the one who paid the price of our redemption that we might be sons of God. That is a marvelous thought.

The church is the family of God. Those who are in the church are in the family of God, and God is their Father. Since all who are in the church have the same Father, they are brothers and sisters to each other. Peter once said to Jesus, "Lo, we have left all, and followed thee. And Jesus answered and said, Verily I say unto you, There is no man that hath left house, or brethren, or sisters, or father, or mother, or wife, or children, or lands, for my sake, and the gospel's, but he shall receive an hundredfold now in this time, houses, and brethren, and sisters, and mothers, and children, and lands, with persecutions; and in the world to come eternal life." (Mark 10:28-30.) Peter had given up his fishing business, and he did not have material possessions. He could say to a lame man, "Silver and gold have I none." He, along with other disciples was despised, scourged, beaten, and ridiculed, but Christ promised that he and others would receive now, in this present world a hundredfold. That is not twofold, which would be twice as much as one gave. A hundredfold is a hundred times as much as one gives. That is what Jesus promised, but He was not talking of dollars. He said "houses, and brethren, and sisters, and mothers, and lands, with persecution, and in the world to come eternal life." If one gives up much to follow Jesus, he will not be a loser. He will have many people who will be as brothers and sisters to him. He will have spiritual possessions of far more value than those things he gave up. I have many homes where I know my place at the table and where I feel welcome to spend the night. My mothers and sisters and brethren live there.

I talk often with people who say, "I don't think you have to be in the church." Forgetting for a moment all other considerations, let me ask in return, "Why would any one want to stay out of the church?" There are brethren and sisters and mothers and children in the church, and they can share with you every blessing that they have received from the Lord. I do not want to miss having all those relatives. My father and mother had only one son, but I have many brothers and sisters in the family of God that are as near and dear to me as I believe physical brothers and sisters could be. The church of the Lord Jesus Christ is the greatest family on earth. No civic club to which you might belong could in any way compare with it. Do you know of anything better than to be a child of God and a brother to Jesus Christ? In times of sickness when we have been as much as five or six hundred miles from our physical parents, we have had mothers, fathers, brothers, and sisters in the church who have done far more for us than we could ever dream of being able to repay. We learn in the family of God to bear one another's burdens.

Jesus said, "A new commandment I give unto you, That ye love one another; as I have loved you, that ye also love one another. By this shall all men know that ye are my disciples, if ye have love one to another." (John 13:34, 35.) The world can recognize us as disciples of Christ if we act like brothers and sisters and have proper love for one another. "We know that we have passed from death unto life, because we love the brethren. He that loveth not his brother abideth in death." (1 John 3:14.) Do you really love your brother? Your answer determines whether or not you are walking in the truth. Sometimes brethren in a business meeting of the church cannot talk over some problem without getting angry with one another, raising their voices, yelling at each other, and being harsh and bitter. I think brothers should be able to work together in a better way than that. The church is the family of God, and the members ought to act like children in that family and not act in ways that bring reproach upon the church. They ought to treat one another as brethren, even the weak members. They ought to have special interest in the weak brother just as in the physical family each member would be expected to show special care for the sick one. If one is in distress, others should go to his rescue. Paul compares the spiritual body of Christ, which is the church, to our own physical bodies. He shows that each member has his particular function to perform and all are needed. Then the body is one perfect whole with no schism in it. Each member has a special care for every other member. "And whether one member suffer, all the members suffer with it; or one member be honored, all the members rejoice with it." (1 Cor. 12:14-26.)

We are heirs of God. Peter said that we have an "inheritance incorruptible, and undefiled, and that fadeth not away, reserved in heaven for you, who are kept by the power of God through faith unto salvation ready to be revealed in the last time." (1 Peter 1:4,5.) We do not have anything on earth like that. Heaven has something that earth cannot offer. Everything that belongs to this life will perish. Even the earth itself will be burned up, and nothing that has been laid up here will be of any lasting value. Heaven offers an inheritance to its heirs that is incorruptible, and undefiled, and that fadeth not away. Since we are heirs of God, we have this inheritance reserved for us, and we have no fear that moths or rust will destroy it or that a thief will break through and steal it. It is kept safe for all of us who are kept by the power of God through faith. We have hope of receiving it when this life is over. Hope is desire based on expectation. The Lord has promised the inheritance, and we rely on His word, so we hope to receive it. This hope which we have is an "anchor of the soul, both sure and stedfast, and which entereth into that within the vail." (Heb. 6:19.)

The church is spoken of as the bride of Christ. He is the bridegroom. We are familiar with those words. To show the relationship between Christ and His church Paul used the figure of the husband and wife. "Wives, submit yourselves unto your own husbands, as unto the Lord. For the husband is the head of the wife, even as Christ is the head of the church: and he is the saviour of the body. Therefore as the church is subject unto Christ, so let the wives be to their own husbands in everything. Husbands, love your wives, even as Christ also loved the church, and gave himself for it." (Eph. 5:22-25.)

In using the physical relationship of husband and wife as a type of the spiritual relationship of Christ and the church, we can better understand the closeness that exists between them. The husband is the head of the wife, so he makes the laws for the home. The wife is to obey him in all things, but her obedience becomes a thing of joy because he loves her and desires the very best for her always. Christ is the head of the church, and He makes the laws for it. The church as His bride must follow carefully every law He gives. There should never be any reason or desire to change what He has said because He loves the church. He gave Himself for it "that he might present it to himself a glorious church, not having spot, or wrinkle, or any such thing; but that it should be holy and without blemish." (Eph. 5:27.)

When John was permitted to see a glimpse of the church in its glorified state, he said, "And I John saw the holy city, new Jerusalem, coming down from God out of heaven, prepared as a bride adorned for her husband." (Rev. 21:2.) As the bridegroom eagerly awaits the coming of his bride in her soft white gown and pure loveliness, so Christ awaits the coming of His bride who will be without spot and without wrinkle and without blemish.

One of the most beautiful words in our language is the word "home" because at the end of a long, weary day the members of it can find rest and comfort. Heaven will be an eternal home, a place of rest, of happiness, and peace. There the gates are of pearl and the street of pure gold. There God and the Lamb lighten the city so that there is no need of the sun or moon. "And God shall wipe away all tears from their eyes; and there shall be no more death, neither sorrow, nor crying, neither shall there be any more pain: for the former things are passed away. And he that sat upon the throne said, Behold, I make all things new." (Rev. 21:4,5a.)

Chapter 14

CONCLUSION

When we voice our concern over the breakdown of our American home life, we may be accused of being pessimistic, uninformed, or overly critical. There have always been unhappy homes and disobedient children. That is true, but a person would have to close his eyes and stop his ears not to realize that there are more divorces, more delinquent children, and more youthful criminals than ever before in the history of our country.

Preachers over the years have been concerned with the problems that threaten the home, and they have tried to awaken sleeping husbands, wives, and parents to their duties to one another and to their children. If we cannot arouse them to their duties, the decay of the homes will bring about a downfall of our nation. We have been told repeatedly that one contributing cause of the fall of the Roman Empire was the breakdown of the home.

Some parents, grandparents, and others are waking up, looking around, becoming deeply concerned, and are trying to remedy the situation. I have a file of articles which I have collected through the years on many subjects by many preachers and other writers. In looking through some that I have on various aspects of the home, its relationships, and its problems I ran across a letter that came to me several years ago when I was editing a small religious journal. The writer sent two subscriptions to the paper, one to be sent to a son and the other to a sister-in-law. It shows so clearly what has happened in one home, which is only a sample of what is happening in thousands of homes over our nation, that I want to share it with you.

I shall change the names to protect the identity of those mentioned.

After giving the information concerning the subscriptions requested, the letter continues:

"My reason for sending these is my concern for their spiritual welfare. Maybe they will read something that will bring them to the realization of the irresponsible rut that they have drifted into.

"John is my only child, and he has a son five years old. My daughter-in-law is one of the very best. They are both members of the Lord's church.

"They both work eight hours a day and sometimes more. The routine is this: He leaves at 5:00 A.M. and eats breakfast at his place of work. She leaves at 7:30 A.M. They come home about 5:30 P.M. They are both so tired that they are not even kind to little Johnny. Television is the center of their lives while they are home. I had to ask for it to be turned down so that I could offer thanks before we ate. They watch it until every one is nodding. There is no time to hear what the child wants to tell. There is no time for the reading of God's word. No time for prayer.

"The girl who is hired to do the work and care for the child smokes and uses foul language. She and her cousin spend the evening in a night club. They come in from 11:00 P.M. to 2:00 A.M. almost every night.

"When the weekend comes they are all in a nervous condition for the lack of rest. On Saturday morning they sleep late. Johnny has no attention. They are all too busy getting ready to go bowling in the afternoon. Then there is a late picture at the theater down town. On Sunday morning breakfast is eaten about 11:00. Following that there is the laundry to do, and the car is to be washed. Everything must be prepared for work on Monday morning. There is no time for worship. The child is given no consideration.

"Everybody smokes like a furnace. My reason for writing this story is to put before you the situation that exists among those who are more interested in self-satisfaction than in their duty to children or to God. John and Sue became Christians while they were both young. The influence of those around them has made its mark. When they took me to worship they did not partake of the Lord's Supper. Then I knew that they feel guilty.

"If you have material to publish in your paper which would awake people to their responsibility to children and to God, maybe, just maybe, they might take heed and Johnny would learn about God before it is too late. He plays 'cowboys' and enjoys all the glory of guns and killing. Although my heart was heavy I did not press the issue because it was my first visit since they were married six years ago. They were in a distant state for five years.

"To my knowledge they do not drink or go to dances. They seem to love each other very much. I would never say or do anything to cause discord.

"My sister-in-law is a person who is to be pitied. She has a ten year old son. He has never been in a house of worship in his life. If only she could realize that she will be held accountable for her neglect, in failing to live where she could attend worship and teach him the scriptures. I believe this is her greatest sin. She is an affectionate mother, an excellent 'keeper at home,' and a decent person. Her husband drank and failed his responsibility as a father and a husband. She was left with the child to care for and feels lost. If only she could see that God has not forsaken her and that her responsibility is no less because she has been mistreated. She is a member of the church, but she has been listening to sermons lately by a Christian Scientist. I am very concerned about her.

"This may be the situation in other homes. Maybe others would be helped by sermons that are printed for the purpose of making them understand that God has told us what our duty is to him and that worldly things can cause us to lose our souls.

"May God help you to ever stand for the truth, in the world of false teachers. We need more who would contend for the truth."

That ends the letter, and we can weep with this parent who has such a burden on his heart. I do not know what conditions existed in the home when the son was growing to manhood. I do not know what mistakes were made in the training or lack of training that he received. I do not know whether he has changed his ways or whether he is allowing his child to continue to grow up in a totally irreligious environment. The case is by no means isolated. There are thousands of homes where the same conditions exist. We wondered together in an earlier chapter why we lose so many of our children. The letter explains one or two cases. Parents are indifferent to their duties. There is no time for the children. They are too often left to the vulgar, smoking irresponsible baby sitter. The writer asked that there be more sermons printed that would deal with the problems facing the homes, and we tried to comply with the request. I stop and ask myself however, how much good was done by the articles. If there was no time to give to the child, and if television was the shrine before which the family worshiped, I doubt seriously that religious papers would be read. They would merely clutter the wastebasket.

I think there should be more sermons preached in the pulpits and more written in papers that go into homes. We should realize that the Bible deals with every aspect of our lives, and the whole counsel should be taught. How can we reach those who will not sit in the pews when the sermons are being preached, and who will not read when the sermons come in written form into their homes? How can we wake parents to their responsibilities? Many preachers and teachers have tried and are still trying, and even if they succeed in only discharging their own duty, the time will not be wasted.

We are not faced with new problems. There are just more of the same old problems.   July 1960 I found an article in *Searching the Scriptures,* a religious journal of great value to those who will read it, that I considered worthy of keeping and sharing with others. It has this note by the editor at the beginning:

"The following article was written by brother Rufus Clifford and appeared in the *Gospel Guardian,* June 2, 1949. Eleven years later the situation has grown worse, and we are now more in need of this study than at the time it was written."

After sixteen more years have passed and we look around us, it is evident that the situation has worsened still more, and we need to read it again. It repeats in another's words some of the same principles that we have mentioned in other chapters, but they will bear repeating. The author, Rufus Clifford, called it "The Disintegration of American Home-Life." That is the problem that we have concerned ourselves with in this entire little book that we are bringing to you. Let us examine the article:

"There has been a break-down in the homes of America. Our homes have become dressing rooms, filling stations, and beer parlors. Moral corruption has flooded the land.

"Juvenile delinquency is one of our major problems.

The FBI reported recently a steady increase in crime, year by year, with teen-agers responsible for a very substantial portion of it. In 1945, for example, there was an increase of 12.4% in crime over 1944; the upsurge in crime being the biggest since 1930.

"A survey of 543,892 arrests records showed that 17 year-olds lead all others in the number of arrests, with 18 year-olds following a close second. Arrests of girls under 21 more than doubled in 1945 over 1941. A rape, felonious assault, or killing occurred in our country every 6.4 seconds. Youths under 21 years of age accounted for 51% of all automobile thefts, 42% of all burglaries, and 28% of all robberies.

"What is the cause of all these increases? There has been a catastrophic break-down in the homes of our country. For the most part, delinquent parents can be said to be the cause of delinquent children. Juvenile delinquency is only the symptom of a disease which is eating away the very foundations of our country, and is threatening to destroy the church of the Lord. That disease is a lack, a dearth of truly Christian homes.

"Roger Babson says any hunt for a solution to the problem of juvenile delinquency must start with the reconstruction of parenthood and its untransferable duties. A wayward youngster and an erring parent are usually but the opposite sides of the same bad coin. Child hoodlumism will end only when legal and financial responsibility is acknowledged not only in the realm of feeding, housing, and clothing, but in the much more important realm of training and teaching.

"Judge Sam Davis Tatum, judge of the Juvenile and Domestic Relations Court of Davidson County, Tennessee, reported recently that of the 9,500 boys under 17 who had come into the courts of Davidson County, there was not one whose parents went to Bible classes and church services regularly. He further stated that there were only 44 boys of the 9,500 who themselves went to Sunday school and church services regularly.

"It is clear that we have over-emphasized the material things to the neglect of spiritual things. The United States of America in 1942 spent in all religious enterprises the sum of $721,000,000.00; this is less than 1% of our national income. In that same year the American people spent $5,200,000,000.00 for alcoholic drinks and an additional $2,400,000,000.00 for tobacco. Thus, for whiskey and tobacco the American people spent in that year more than ten times the sum spent on all religious endeavors of every description. And the awful contrast continues to grow even more shameful and disgraceful in the years following the war. In 1946 approximately $10,800,000,000.00 was spent by Americans for whiskey and tobacco; while only about $4,000,000,000.00 was spent in all our educational institutions, from kindergartens through universities.

"There are over 437,000 saloons in America—one for every 300 people. To each five church buildings in the nation, there are seven saloons. There are 27,000,000 young people in America who are receiving no religious instruction of any kind whatsoever. And of this number approximately 16,000,000 have never been inside any kind of church building even one time! There are 60,000,000 Americans who profess no religion of any kind.

"Any one curious about the evident decline in national morals, including all the problems of delinquency both juvenile and adult, need look no further. The figure denoting comparative interests and evaluations tell the story; they speak for themselves. When whiskey and tobacco are more important to a nation than all her churches and schools, the fall of that nation surely cannot be long postponed.

"There has been an alarming decline in the moral character of the womanhood of our nation. We are witnessing the disgusting sight of cigarette smoking, paint-smearing, cocktail drinking women, reeling drunkenly in the streets of our cities and towns. In 1920 one woman was arrested for drunkenness to every five men arrested for that cause. In 1946 the ratio had risen to one woman for each two men. In 1949 the proportion is approximately even.

"Women have left the homes, where God ordained they should be, and have gone out into the world to compete with men in the store, the factory and the office. They have left their children in the hands of maids and 'baby-sitters' instead of caring for them themselves. Divorce and immorality on an unprecedented scale have come in the wake of such behavior.

"It is inevitable that these conditions in the home life should reflect themselves in the church. The church in many places has been filled up with worldly minded people, irreverent, and flippant in their attitudes. The word of God has been disregarded and lightly set aside.

"The home is the training center for the church. It is nearly impossible for one reared in a home filled with irreverence and disregard for God's law to grow up to become the kind of Christian and the kind of citizen he ought to be. We must build homes in which piety, reverence for God and spiritual things are stressed and impressed. Then we will have better communities in which to live, and better churches with which to sound out the gospel of Jesus Christ into all the earth."

That juvenile delinquency is a parental problem, few right-thinking people would deny. Parents will have to give an account for the way they bring up their children. Proper teaching, proper discipline, and proper love would correct most of the evils among the young. The early years of life are years of learning. Young people learn their lessons well. If they are taught reverence, respect, and love for God, the juvenile delinquent problems would be solved. If they are taught a lack of reverence, respect, and love, they will become problems to the home, the community in which they live, to the church, and to the nation as a whole. If they are not taught the proper things in the home, they will imbibe the evil examples there and from their associates in the world. Parents are responsible for the training, the environment, and the development of their children. Discipline is the key word. It means proper guidance. Children need guidelines and the proper restraint exercised on the part of the parents that will keep them in those guidelines.

Ours is not the only generation that has been disturbed with juvenile problems. In a very brief article lifted from *Sword of Peace,* August 1960, John Iverson showed that juvenile delinquency was not new in that year, but was a problem of long standing. It is certainly not new in our day, nor is it diminishing as the years pass. Let me give you this picture of trouble in the days of the Old Testament period of the judges.

"Do you think 'juvenile delinquency' is an evil that is peculiar to our day? If so, then you would do well to read your Bible, particularly such passages as are found in the book of First Samuel.

"Eli was judge in Israel and priest of the living God.

When he grew old, instead of his children's being a source
of joy to that religious leader of olden days, they caused
him much heartache and grief. After Eli had heard of the
almost unimaginable sins which his sons had committed,
as recorded in 1 Samuel 2:22, he said unto them, 'Why do
you such things? for I hear of your evil dealings by all this
people ... it is no good report that I hear: ye make the
Lord's people to transgress.'

"What a tragedy! The sons of this 'man of God' were a
stumbling block to the Lord's people! However, the sons
(though vile and wicked indeed) were not altogether to
blame, for we are told in 1 Samuel 3:13, 'For I have told
him that I will judge his house forever for the iniquity
which he knoweth; because his sons made themselves vile,
and he *restrained them not.*' Eli did not curb his children;
he apparently just let them have their own way. Perhaps
he had the idea that 'boys will be boys.' Yes, but those
boys grew up to be men—'vile' men! This case alone
should be enough to convince all parents that placing the
necessary restrictions upon our children is needful if we
expect them to grow up to be *useful* citizens and individuals whose manner of life will be worthy of the gospel of
Christ. Think on these things."

Parents take for granted that their children will turn out
all right. Too many Christians suppose that their children
are listening to the sermons to which they are exposed
regularly, that they are studying their lessons that are
assigned by their class teachers, and that they are watching the good examples set before them. They forget that
there must be teaching done in the home. Children are not
capable of being entirely on their own in the matter of
study. They must be taught.

Other preachers in other years have realized the need for
more teaching in order to warn parents who are asleep at
their posts. Clifford Payne wrote in *The Gospel Advocate*
on November 12, 1959 an article which he called "Present
Perils of Growing Up." He, too, makes reference to some
things that we have already had occasion to mention. We
need to realize that the problems are many, but with the
proper awareness of their seriousness we could do more to
combat them. The article follows:

"Some interesting but alarming facts about juvenile delinquency in New Mexico were recently released through
the press. Juvenile delinquency increased sixty-five

percent from 1955 to 1958—from 8,158 to 13,388 cases. It was also noted that the average delinquent is a boy fifteen years old. (*The New Mexican,* September 28, 1959, page 12.) It is likely that other states have noticed a similar rise in juvenile delinquency.

"The problems confronting the young people of our age are so prevalent and pernicious that they cause us to tremble and to engage in sober reflection. We dare not be satisfied with the status quo, for we cannot permit our youth to be sacrificed to a godless age. Yet we are inclined to wonder: Who has the correct answers? Who can really speak with authority? But on the other hand, are we going to say that the problems are insoluble? Surely not, because that would be abandonment to utter pessimism. As in past ages, the Bible has the answers to the perplexing and intricate juvenile problems of the twentieth century.

"Doubtless some are not too familiar with the various adverse forces plaguing the young of today. If we are to properly combat these forces, we must be aware of their existence and nature.

"*School and Infidelity.* Although it is indicative of a regrettably deteriorated state, young people frequently hear Christianity and the Bible berated by instructors in our public schools. When Christianity is subtilely or openly attacked by teachers—those who represent learning and leadership to the students—the results are incalculably detrimental, even to the students who are strongest spiritually. Knowing that this situation exists and that it is worsening, Christian parents and teachers must graphically warn our young people that modernistic and atheistic teachers simply express their own opinions when denouncing things sacred. Such denunciatory expressions are not to be gullibly accepted as truth. The young person who is prone to question assertions which are opposed to his religious training at home and at church is less likely to be victimized. This characteristic is admirable for the old as well as the young. (Col. 2:8.)

"*Literature and Lasciviousness.* The preponderance of salacious literature circulating in this country is enough in itself to effect the complete ruination of the younger generation. Trashy, vitiating literature is no longer confined to smut peddlers, but it is found on the shelves of public libraries. Do not many of the best sellers abound in lascivious and immoral passages, which purportedly are only realistic and/or naturalistic in design? Young people have complete access to these books, and, because adult readers have made them best sellers, they feel justified in imbibing their polluting contents. For many years the world has known a type of realistic and naturalistic litera- ture, but the naturalism of Maupassant and Zola is mild compared to that of Lawrence and O'Hara. Not only is the mind corrupted by the pronography of these modern novels, but youth is imperiled by the deceit of them also. It is imperative that youth understand that the promiscu- ous way of life depicted is not as predominant and gen- erally accepted as the reader is led to believe. Society still strongly deprecates such conduct. The unfortunate truth is that these novels do not accurately depict life in general as much as they set the stage for and encourage evil living.

"*Travel and Environment.* Admittedly it sounds almost incredible to the younger generation, but until relatively recently the environment of one town or city was largely the molding influence of its young. Modern transporta- tion, however, has forever removed that simplicity from our society. If the youth of the past were molded by the environment of one locality, the youth of today find al- most the opposite true. Present transportation affords one the ability to find the kind of environment which best suits his fancy. This particular aspect of our modern age can be utilized for good or evil. But, unhappily, its evil possibilities are being exploited in no small way.

"*Lawlessness Often Unpunished.* Noting the enormity of unsolved crimes, both petty and major, some now ques- tion the validity of the contention that 'crime does not pay.' It is simply natural for juvenile delinquency to in- crease when lawlessness often seems to go unpunished. Doubtless young people at times fail to observe that there are ways of paying for a crime, other than by being appre- hended by the police. One should not be misled by what occasionally appear to be successful acts of crime, for it remains true that 'the way of transgressors is hard.' (Prov. 13:15.)

"It is suggested that at least two facts can be concluded from what has been said. First, although growing up has always been a painful and hazardous process, modern con- ditions tend to make it even more difficult. Secondly, present conditions make detrimental influences outside the home stronger than ever.

"It is to be remembered that, whether good or evil, teaching and environment will always mold one's life. (Prov. 22:6; 1 Cor. 15:33.) With this in mind we offer four suggestions which, if followed, should successfully combat the adverse forces faced by the young.

"Unquestionably the home should be sincerely and thoroughly Christian. (2 Tim. 1:5; 3:14,15.) Fortified by the teaching and atmosphere of a Christian home, the young person is well equipped to withstand those evil forces which cannot always be evaded. The bonds of love and comradeship between parent and child should be unbreakable and enduring. For this relationship to exist, parents must command respect and manifest an interest in that which concerns their children. The children then feel that they can place complete confidence in their parents. Furthermore, of utmost significance is that the parents occupy the position of authority, for the youngster who sees this will feel much closer to and have greater respect for his parents. Let us endeavor in every way possible to make the home life of the young conducive to bringing 'them up in the nurture and admonition of the Lord.' (Eph. 6:4.)

"The church has much to offer in strengthening our youth if only we give it a chance to function fully. But when indifferent parents, or parents who are seemingly insensible to any juvenile problem, take little interest in seeing that their children are faithful to the various Bible classes designed for them, the wonderful influence which the church could wield is sharply curtailed. That parents will soon awaken to their responsibility in this matter is something eminently worthy of our prayers.

"The writer has personally witnessed the apostasy of several Christian young people, caused mainly by the unwholesome environment of certain state universities and the relentless antichristian instruction of some professors. This tragedy is widespread; consequently, Christian education should be unceasingly promoted by all Christian parents. Irrespective of what may be said in the negative, it has been undeniably evinced that Christian education is a most effective bulwark against many of the evils which threaten youth. Indeed the splendid environment of our Christian colleges by itself makes the colleges infinitely worthwhile.

"Finally, clearly defined standards of right and wrong should be kept before young people. It is becoming increasingly more obvious that when these standards are obscured or destroyed, young people become confused and insecure, which facilitates moral laxity. The Bible contains the proper standards; therefore, it should be their basic textbook.

"How shall the young secure their hearts,
    And guard their lives from sin?
Thy word the choicest rules imparts
    To keep the conscience clean.

"The hour is late, and there is little time to waste! Our young people will not grow up to be fine Christians and citizens by accident. It will take dedication and work by adults. Let us resolve to do everything within our power to prepare them to be useful in the Lord's church in the challenging years to come."

If our homes were God-fearing homes, there would be fewer youthful criminals and fewer problems of various kinds. The homes would be places that build character and instill the principles of right and wrong in the hearts of the children. What are God-fearing homes? To answer the question, I want to do so in the words of Lynn Headrick. In the October 1959 issue of *Sword of Peace,* he wrote an article which he called "God-Fearing Homes." I give my whole-hearted endorsement of his definition.

"The Bible says that Cornelius 'feared God with all his house.' (Acts 10:2.) If only that could be said of all homes! It is evident to all that there are many unhappy and broken homes in every place. There is hardly an individual but that has a friend or a relative whose home is anything but a God-fearing one. The purpose of this article is to help us have God-fearing homes.

"God-fearing homes form the foundation of a well-ordered society. Infidelity, moral corruption, juvenile and adult delinquency, and all sorts of vice spring from homes where the fear of God is not observed. But what does it mean to fear God? You will, as a student of the Old Testament, remember that God told Abraham to offer his son Isaac as a burnt offering. Abraham did not question God's pronouncement. His faith in God caused him to place Isaac upon the altar. Then Abraham 'stretched forth his hand, and took the knife to slay his son.' Here is a demon-

stration of implicit obedience to God. At this point an
angel of the Lord stayed the hand of Abraham and said,
'Now I know that thou fearest God.' (Gen. 22:12.) This
illustration teaches us that to fear God is to obey God.
What are you doing toward making your home a God-
fearing home? Let us now notice the home life of some
Bible characters in order to better know what a God-
fearing home is and also what it is not.

"Timothy was 'the son of a Jewess that believed; but
his father was a Greek.' (Acts 16:1.) In our day there are
many young men whose conduct is such that they get a
bad reputation in the community in which they live. Such
was not the case with Timothy. It is refreshing to note
that Timothy 'was well reported of by the brethren that
were of Lystra and Iconium.' (Acts 16:2.) In our day the
newspapers are filled with reports of young men who are
leading profligate, gangster-type lives, having little
regard for things spiritual. If only all young men would
imitate Timothy of whom Paul said, 'that from a babe
thou hast known the sacred writings which are able to
make thee wise unto salvation through faith which is in
Christ Jesus.' (2 Tim. 3:15.) What better thing can a child
know than 'the sacred writings'? And who took the time
and effort required to teach the word of God to this child
Timothy? Faith comes by hearing the word of God, and
Paul said that he was 'reminded of the unfeigned faith'
which was in Timothy. Timothy, your faith dwelt first in
'thy grandmother Lois and thy mother Eunice.' (2 Tim.
1:5.) Yes, Timothy was taught by his mother and grandmother. Every little 'Timothy' today needs a 'grandmother Lois' and a 'mother Eunice.' If Lois and Eunice
were alive today and had the responsibility of teaching a
Timothy I do not believe that they would blow cigarette
smoke in his face or allow curse words to proceed from
their mouths for a little fellow to imitate. I do not believe
that they would allow Timothy to feed his young mind on
comic books protraying all sorts of vice. I do not think
that they would be proud of the fact that their Timothy
could name more 'movie stars' than Bible characters. I do
not believe that Eunice and Lois, if they were alive today,
would laugh when little Timothy drew a toy pistol and
shot 'the outlaw down' or poked his fist in the face of a
neighbor boy in imitation of some television 'hero.' On the
contrary, Eunice and Lois would do all in their power to

fill the mind of the child with the 'golden rule' and instruct
him by precept and example in 'the sacred writings which
are able to make thee wise unto salvation through faith
which is in Christ Jesus.' May God give all parents
wisdom to train their children in the way they should go.
Constant effort will be required for this great task.

"'If only I could marry a king or a rich man!' Some
young ladies have perhaps entertained such a thought in
their hearts. Money, pleasure, and gaiety are associated
with kings' houses and perhaps this is the reason for such
thoughts and desires. But God-fearing homes are built on
a much better and surer foundation. Rather than thinking
of marrying one with plenty of money and who can
provide earthly pleasures, one should think of marrying
one that will help in providing the proper spiritual atmosphere. King Solomon 'made silver to be in Jerusalem as
stones.' (1 Kings 10:27.) 'All king Solomon's drinking
vessels were of gold.' (v. 21.) They did not use empty pea-
nut butter jars for drinking glasses. Solomon had 'seven
hundred wives, princesses, and three hundred concu-
bines.' (1 Kings 11:3.) Some one is wont to say, 'Oh, for
the life of Solomon!' But sober thought will say, 'What
tragedy!' Solomon's 'wives turned away his heart after
other gods; and his heart was not perfect with Jehovah his
God.' (1 Kings 11:4.) Solomon's home was not a God-
fearing home for at least two reasons: (1) He violated
God's law of one man for one woman and one woman for
one man until death separated them. (cf. Matt. 19:5,6.)
(2) His home served not the God of heaven but rather
served idols. If our home is living in rebellion to God's law
of marriage or if our home is living in rebellion to God's
law of service then we do not have a God-fearing home.

"The God-fearing home is the happy home. It holds
'forth the word of life' 'in the midst of a crooked and per-
verse generation.' It is indeed a picture beautiful to behold. Strive to have a God-fearing home."

God-fearing homes could change the morals of our country and return them to the level that the Lord intended.
Homes are the very basic units of society, and we must
guard them carefully lest we allow them to disintegrate to
such an extent that they will bring about the downfall of
our nation. Nations fall when they decay from within.

Homes will be what God intended for them to be when
each member of the family which comprises the homes are

living as God intended. The husband is to exercise his God-given authority as the head of the home. He is to be an instructor of his children, bringing "them up in the nurture and admonition of the Lord." He is to provide for their physical, mental, moral, and spiritual welfare. Some men *shift* rather than *shoulder* their obligations as provider. A man must be a restrainer of his children as well as a provider. Some one has said that he learned some valuable lessons at the knees of his mother and *across* the knees of his father. Solomon said, "He that spareth the rod hateth his son; but he that loveth him chasteneth him betimes." (Prov. 13:24.)

Some would have us believe that if we use the rod of correction on the child we will warp his personality. Frankly, I have seen some personalities that needed warping! Solomon said also, "Foolishness is bound up in the heart of a child, but the rod of correction will drive it far from him." (Prov. 22:15.) Again, he said, "Correct thy son, and he will give thee rest; yea, he will give delight unto thy soul." (Prov. 29:17.)

If we do not want to weep the bitter tears of shame, remorse, and regret in the days to come we must wake up and restrain our children while there is still hope of saving them.

A woman must stay in her God-assigned place of subjection to her husband if she would please the Lord. She must fulfill her duties to her husband and be a worthy keeper at home. There is no more noble work that a woman can do than that of guiding the house and caring for her children. When a woman becomes a wife, bears children, and helps to bring them up in the nurture and admonition of the Lord, she has found the place in the home that the Lord wants her to fill.

Children have their own places to fill in the home, and parents have the responsibility of seeing that they fill them in the right way. I have an article on file which I took from *Sword of Peace*, October 1959. It was written by Gene Robinson, and he called it "Children and the Home." It sums up some of the things we said in our chapter on the child's place in the home. Read it with me, if you will.

"An inalienable right that every person has is to be born into a Christian family. But how few enjoy such a distinction! Many volumes have been written by psychologists,

and a great number of philosophies have found their way
into our thinking about home life. But none of these are of
any value unless they harmonize with Bible teaching. The
word of God has given us all things that pertain to life and
godliness (2 Pet. 1:3), and certainly the relationship of
parent and child is one of them. No better statement of
this relationship can be found than that which is found in
Ephesians 6:1-4. Children, obey your parents in the
Lord: for this is right. Honor thy father and mother
(which is the first commandment with promise), that it
may be well with thee, and thou mayest live long on the
earth. And, ye fathers, provoke not your children to
wrath: but nurture them in the chastening and admonition
of the Lord.' It is significant that in verse 2 both mother
and father are mentioned in connection with honor and in
verse 4 only the father is mentioned in connection with the
upbringing of the child. This fact seems to stress the truth
that the father is head of the house (Eph. 5:23) and is primarily responsible for the training of the children, a position that a vast number of men have long since abdicated
or from which they have been forced into exile. A father
cannot very well nurture his children according to the dic-
tates of the Lord if he is subject to their mother! Crude
and feeble jokes have been made concerning this relatio-
ship, but in many quarters it is all too true.

"I would not minimize the God-given position of Christian motherhood, for it is indeed a coveted one. What a joy
it must be to give life to one of God's beings and to be the
helpmeet of his father in directing his life into channels
where he, too, can present his body a living sacrifice.
(Rom. 12:1,2.) Much must be accomplished before the
child reaches the time of accountability and much there-
after. There is the initial period of training when the parents must instill principles of right and wrong into the
child. For this period of training there is no substitute.
Seeing that the child is in a class on Sunday morning and
Wednesday night is important, and he should be taught
the importance of it; but at this age nearly all of his training should be in the home by the *father* and *mother* and
not by a maid or baby-sitter while the father and mother
are away at work. A child grows into maturity having become a product of that which he has been taught. Many
have the misconception that if a child grows up through
years of disobedience and delinquency into a social and

spiritual misfit, it is because of 'bad blood,' something inherited from his grandparents, aunts, uncles, or some other relative for whom one or both parents do not particularly care. Such a view would hold God responsible for having created a 'bad' person. But inasmuch as God created man in His own image (Gen. 1:27), man is not created bad but grows into it by what he is taught. Human beings do not inherit bad traits. They are taught them. The whole point is this: Man is a product of his teaching. 'Train up a child in the way he should go, and even when he is old he will not depart from it.' (Prov. 22:6.) Lamenting mothers and fathers spend many hours feeling sorry for themselves wondering what has happened to their sons and daughters. A few years ago a young man of tender years was in a Bible class I was teaching. He was alert, studious, and as far as I know completely faithful. His father was out of duty entirely and his mother was lukewarm. Soon the young man followed their example and is now serving the devil twenty four hours a day. A few months ago the father pleaded with me to try to reach the boy. My efforts failed. Train up a child ...? This father knows he did not. The amazing part of the story is this: the father is still out of duty and the mother still lukewarm, but they continue to plead for some one to try to reach their son! No, there is absolutely no substitute for godly parents. Most likely faithful Christian parents will have faithful children.

"Not only do young people need the teaching of parents, their association and example of godliness, but many times they need their counsel. The majority of problems of young people as far as adults are concerned, are relatively trivial; but to them the problems are real. They are complex and exasperating and should be counseled as though they might change the course of history. If young people are not given counsel by their parents, they are going to turn to some other source, and it very well could be the wrong source. Closely associated with counseling is guidance. And certainly discipline will fall into this category. From way back in the history of God's people we read of disciplinary problems, and one of the most vivid is the story of the sons of Eli. They were base men who knew not Jehovah (1 Sam. 2:12), and the cause might well be found in the fact that he 'restrained them not.' (1 Sam. 3:13.) Fruits of laxity toward discipline can readily be seen in the mob violence and gang wars of recent days in New

York. Those who cannot understand why their children grow into rebellious and disobedient adults are parents who provided them no other way in which to go. Paul said to Timothy, 'Take heed to thyself, and to thy teaching. Continue in these things: for in doing this thou shalt save both thyself and them that hear thee.' (1 Tim. 4:16.) I trust that parents realize that the 'them that hear thee' also applies to their children.

"It is not uncommon for parents to be so ambitious for the success of their children that they will overlook the fact that 'a man's life consisteth not in the abundance of the things which he possesseth.' (Lk. 12:15.) Somehow it is difficult not to lose sight of true success. Perhaps a portion of the counsel that God gave to Joshua will give us insight as to the meaning of true success. 'This book of the law shall not depart out of thy mouth, and thou shalt meditate thereon day and night, that thou mayest observe to do according to all that is written therein: for then thou shalt make thy way prosperous, and then thou shalt have good success.' (Josh. 1:8.) An education is important in this competitive nation, but the gaining of wealth, acclaim, and social status are a poor and costly substitute for true success. Christ grew mentally, physically, socially, and spiritually. To be successful, the spiritual side of the individual's development cannot be neglected, and this responsibility lies squarely upon the shoulders of parents.

"One last thought: Parents, let your children know that they are loved. It is in no sense unmanly for a father to show affection for his children by telling them that he loves them. In fact, it is criminal if he does not. Parents are the stewards of a priceless possession—children."

One final article I want to share with you. This one first appeared in the *Firm Foundation*, July 14, 1959. It came to me by way of *Gospel Digest*, October 1959. It is entitled "Abuse of Authority in the Home," and it was written by George W. Allison.

"The right kind of a home is a place in which the woman becomes more womanly and the man becomes more manly. It is a good thing for a man to know that he is a man, for a woman to know that she is a woman, and for a child to know that he is a child. Sad results come when a child fails to recognize his position and becomes disrespectful; when the woman tries to be a half-man, half-woman, disliking her own unique capacities; and when the milk-toast husband fails to rise to the responsibilities which the headship of a household demands.

"It is not an accident that a generation of domineering wives, irresponsible husbands, and disrespectful children have appeared at the same time. The man who cannot rule his wife as God commanded cannot long rule his children. The man who does not have the respect and loving submission of his wife will soon have children who treat him with disrespect. The result is bad for all concerned. Women are cheated if their husbands do not take real leadership and children are cheated even more. Only when the place of authority is accepted by the husband and honored by the wife can the true dignity of both manhood and womanhood be appreciated. The strength of a man's character and the beauty of a woman's character appear most normally when he takes his Bible-given place as leader and she takes her place as helper.

"Authority can be abused. It can be to a man's honor or to his disgrace. It is an abuse of authority for a man to handle his children with harsh revengeful discipline. The Bible plainly commands bodily punishments for a child. 'He that spareth his rod hateth his son; but he that loveth him chasteneth him betimes.' (Prov. 13:24.) Effective discipline must be done in love. Much discipline is only an expression of revenge and offensive to a sense of justice.

"Too many parents tolerate defiance until they are exasperated. They tell the child, 'No!' He defies them. At this time, they should quietly and in complete self-control punish disobedience. Instead, they endure his disobedience until aroused to a keen and bitter vexation, and then they 'let off steam' by punishing the child in a spirit of anger. They have done wrong, and probably the child has been wronged. This same spirit causes a man to take a milk stool to a heifer or a bridle to his team. The same spirit is seen in parents who knock their children about their heads. A boy's head is not a soccer ball. It is not his head that has been padded for punishment. Punish the child, and do it thoroughly, and then put him on your lap and tell him that you love him and why he must learn obedience.

"It is an abuse of authority for a man to force his family into circumstances where they cannot obey God. Some men are 'enemies of the cross of Christ ... whose god is their belly, and whose glory is in their shame, who mind earthly things.' (Phil. 3:19.) They want nothing to do with the church and will deliberately plan to move their families out of contact with the church. Other men are spiritual midgets who do not believe that God will keep His word. They do not believe that God will adequately provide for them if they keep their families close to the fellowship of the church. They will uproot their families and move them into a spiritual desert for a more pleasing pay check. There is no Christian fellowship, no sound, scriptural preaching, no place to continue stedfastly in the apostles' teaching and the breaking of bread. These things are given second place, and money matters are given first place. Yes, the Bible says, 'Wives, be in subjection unto your own husbands.' (Eph. 5:22.) It also says, 'Let every soul be in subjection to the higher powers.' (Rom. 13:1.) But when civil government tries to force a Christian into a position where he must disobey God, then, 'We must obey God rather than men.' (Acts 5:29.) I do not believe that a Christian wife must submit to an unchristian husband when he attempts to force her into circumstances where she cannot obey God. This is an abuse of authority. A husband has no authority to defy God!

"It is an abuse of authority for a man to expect right-doing without exemplifying right-doing. God demands as much morally and spiritually of a man as He does of a woman. God expects a father, in every way, to be an example of spiritual fervency and moral purity, even as his wife is to be. God has one standard of right-doing for both. Cigarette smoking is wrong for a woman! It is dirty, wasteful, rude, and harmful. The same is true for a man. Cursing is wrong for a woman. It is indecent, wicked, and against God. It is just as wrong for a man.

"Any man who sets one standard for his wife and children and another for himself is a hypocrite. He is advocating what he does not practice. Any man who drinks, smokes, and laughs at filth, but does not want his family to act that way is a plain hypocrite. Any man who wants his family to do right and to be Christians, but does not set the pattern, is a slacker and a shirker. He does not deserve a loving family. His family cannot thoroughly respect him. You have no right to expect your boy to be one bit better than you are. If your actions cancel what you have to say, if your children act the way you do, you have not one right to rebuke them or discipline them.

"God needs strong men for heads of families. God needs men of character who will use their authority for His honor. Man, if your home is wrong, you are wrong! You are first of all responsible. Have you misused the place that God has given you? Only God through Christ can make a man what he must be in order to be a good husband and father. May you say with Joshua, '... but as for me and my house, we will serve Jehovah.' (Josh. 24:15.)"

Each generation must learn the will of God and pass on what it learns to the next generation. No child can know right from wrong until he is taught. God has revealed His will for us in all matters that pertain to life and godliness in His word. He has left each person the responsibility of learning that will for himself and of passing it on to others. To parents has been given the special responsibility of seeing that their children are trained in the right way. Moses told the children of Israel: "The secret things belong unto the Lord our God: but those things which are revealed belong unto us and to our children for ever, that we may do all the words of this law." (Deut. 29:29.)

The psalmist expressed the proper attitude toward the responsibility that has been committed to all of us when he said:

"Give ear, O my people, to my law: incline your ears to the words of my mouth. I will open my mouth in a parable: I will utter dark sayings of old: which we have heard and known, and our fathers have told us. We will not hide them from their children, shewing to the generation to come the praises of the Lord, and his strength, and his wonderful works that he hath done. For he established a testimony in Jacob, and appointed a law in Israel, which he commanded our fathers, that they should make known to their children: that the generation to come might know them, even the children which should be born; who should arise and declare them to their children: that they might set their hope in God, and not forget the works of God, but keep his commandments: and might not be as their fathers, a stubborn and rebellious generation; a generation that set not their heart aright, and whose spirit was not stedfast with God." (Ps. 78:1-8.)

Printed in the United States
200034BV00003B/145-420/A